Top Notes

William Shakespeare's

The Merchant of Venice

Study notes for Common Module:
Texts and Human Experiences 2019–2023 HSC

Bruce Pattinson and
Lewis Mitchell

A
FIVE SENSES
PUBLICATION

Five Senses Education Pty Ltd
2/195 Prospect Highway
Seven Hills 2147
New South Wales
Australia

Pattinson, Bruce & Mitchell, Lewis
Top Notes – The Merchant of Venice
ISBN 978-1-76032-210-6

CONTENTS

TOP NOTES SERIES

This series has been created to assist HSC students of English in their understanding of set texts. Top Notes are easy to read, providing analysis of issues and discussion of important ideas contained in the texts.

Particular care has been taken to ensure that students are able to examine each text in the context of the module it has been allocated to.

Each text generally includes:

- Notes on the specific module
- Plot summary
- Character analysis
- Setting
- Thematic concerns
- Language studies
- Essay questions and a modelled response
- Other textual material
- Study practice questions
- Useful quotes

We have covered the areas we feel are important for students in their study of *Texts and Human Experiences* for their Common Module. I am sure you will find these Top Notes useful in your studies of English.

Bruce Pattinson
Series Editor

COMMON MODULE: TEXTS AND HUMAN EXPERIENCES

*"It is quite possible—overwhelmingly probable, one might guess—
that we will always learn more about human life and personality
from novels than from scientific psychology"*

NOAM CHOMSKY

What is the Common Module?

The Common Module set for the 2019–23 HSC is *Texts and Human Experiences*. It is compulsory to study this topic as prescribed by NESA and it is common to all three English courses. Remember: you will be learning how texts reveal individual and collective human experiences. There are no right or wrong answers in this module – it is about how you see and interpret material and engage with it.

In the Common Module you will be analysing one prescribed text and a range of short texts that are related to the idea of human experiences. You will analyse texts not only to investigate the ideas they present about this area but also how they convey these ideas. This means you will be looking closely at the techniques a composer uses to represent his / her messages and shape meaning. You will also be looking at relationships between texts in regard to the experiences you explore. Overall, you will become an expert on texts and the human experience — that is, the different notions people have about human experience and the various ways composers manipulate techniques to communicate their ideas about it.

Specifically you will look at one set text from the following list.

- Doerr, Anthony, *All the Light We Cannot See*
- Lohrey, Amanda, *Vertigo*
- Orwell, George, *Nineteen Eighty-Four*
- Parrett, Favel, *Past the Shallows*
- Dobson, Rosemary 'Young Girl at a Window', 'Over the Hill', 'Summer's End', 'The Conversation', 'Cock Crow', 'Amy Caroline', 'Canberra Morning'
- Slessor, Kenneth 'Wild Grapes', 'Gulliver', 'Out of Time', 'Vesper-Song of the Reverend Samuel Marsden', 'William Street', 'Beach Burial'
- Harrison, Jane, *Rainbow's End*
- Miller, Arthur, *The Crucible*
- Shakespeare, William, *The Merchant of Venice*
- Winton, Tim, *The Boy Behind the Curtain* Chapters: 'Havoc: A Life in Accidents', 'Betsy', 'Twice on Sundays', 'The Wait and the Flow', 'In the Shadow of the Hospital', 'The Demon Shark', 'Barefoot in the Temple of Art'
- Yousafzai, Malala & Lamb, Christina, *I am Malala*
- Daldry, Stephen, *Billy Elliot*
- O'Mahoney, Ivan, *Go Back to Where You Came From* – Series 1, Episodes 1, 2 and 3 and *The Response*
- Walker, Lucy, *Waste Land*

NESA has mandated that students must study a related text as part of the common module, and that this should be part of their in-school assessment. However there is NO LONGER a requirement to write about a related text in the HSC examination itself.

WHAT DOES NESA REQUIRE FOR THE COMMON MODULE?

The NESA documentation of the Common Module: Texts and Human Experiences states that students:

- deepen their understanding of how texts represent individual and collective human experiences;

- examine how texts represent human qualities and emotions associated with, or arising from, these experiences;

- appreciate, explore, interpret, analyse and evaluate the ways language is used to shape these representations in a range of texts in a variety of forms, modes and media;

- explore how texts may give insight into the anomalies, paradoxes and inconsistencies in human behaviour and motivations, inviting the responder to see the world differently, to challenge assumptions, ignite new ideas or reflect personally;

- may also consider the role of storytelling throughout time to express and reflect particular lives and cultures;

- by responding to a range of texts, further develop skills and confidence using various literary devices, language concepts, modes and media to formulate a considered response to texts;

- study one prescribed text and a range of short texts that provide rich opportunities to further explore representations of human experiences illuminated in texts;

- make increasingly informed judgements about how aspects of these texts, for example, context, purpose, structure, stylistic and grammatical features, and form shape meaning;

- select one related text and draw from personal experience to make connections between themselves, the world of the text and their wider world;

- by responding and composing throughout the module, further develop a repertoire of skills in comprehending, interpreting and analysing complex texts;

- examine how different modes and media use visual, verbal and/or digital language elements;

- communicate ideas using figurative language to express universal themes and evaluative language to make informed judgements about texts;

- further develop skills in using metalanguage, correct grammar and syntax to analyse language and express a personal perspective about a text

If this is what is required by NESA, we need to examine the concept of human experience carefully so we can adequately respond in these ways. I would recommend that you read the complete document which is on the NESA web site and can be downloaded in Word or Adobe. Understanding this document is an important step in handling the textual material within the guidelines required — remember you are reading for a purpose and should make notes and highlight ideas as you read so that you can develop these ideas later.

UNDERSTANDING THE COMMON MODULE

What are Human Experiences?

The concept of Human Experiences is at the heart of the Common Module.

Human Experiences are experiences of individuals or a group of people (eg a family, society, or nation) in life. There are a very wide range of human experiences which include but go beyond this list:

- feelings or reactions (momentary or long term): love, hate, anger, joy, fear, disgust
- key milestones or stages: birth, childhood, adulthood, marriage, divorce, death
- culture, belonging and identity
- conformity and rebellion
- innocence and guilt, justice
- freedom and repression
- education, vocation, work, sport, leisure
- attraction to a person, idea, group or cause
- opposition to an idea, cause, political system
- religious faith or belief
- extreme events such as an earthquake, avalanche, tsuanami
- regular events such as walking, eating, singing, dancing, discussing ideas.

The word *experience* seems innately connected to the human condition and it is something we have each day whether a mundane experience that is repetitive, or something new and dramatic which offers challenges and rewards. Experiences can vary greatly in their impact on individuals, groups and countries. One example might be a war that is a negative experience for a whole population while we may experience the wonder of medicine with a new vaccine for a deadly disease that saves millions of people. We need to note that the module asks for 'experiences' ...we are a combination of different experiences and each has a varying impact. One person's problem is another's challenge depending on perspective, skill set, previous experience and ability.

Experiences are widespread and often shared: this is why people tell their stories and these shared experiences form part of our cultural heritage. These experiences often inform, warn and teach across entire cultural groups and many stories are shared across cultures.

DEFINING HUMAN EXPERIENCES

Now let's attempt to define what human experiences are and shape them into a more coherent and easily understood framework so we can begin our investigation at a basic level of understanding before moving into more complex analysis and looking at how the texts illuminate our understanding of the term.

Dictionary.com defines the term **experience** as:

noun

1. a particular instance of personally encountering or undergoing something:

2. the process or fact of personally observing, encountering, or undergoing something:

3. the observing, encountering, or undergoing of things generally as they occur in the course of time:
   to learn from experience; the range of human experience.

4. knowledge or practical wisdom gained from what one has observed, encountered, or undergone, e.g. *a man of experience.*

5. *Philosophy.* the totality of the cognitions given by perception; all that is perceived, understood, and remembered.

verb

(used with object), **experienced, experiencing.**

6. to have experience of; meet with; undergo; feel, e.g. *to experience nausea.*

7. to learn by experience.

idiom

8. **experience religion,** to undergo a spiritual conversion by which one gains or regains faith in God.

Obviously there are a number of definitions according to context, but all are applicable to our study in some shape or form, as the range of human experience is so vast. The search for 'new experience' has driven much of the development of people, groups, cultures and nations over past millennia. New experiences are always met with excitement and often trepidation as to what change they might bring.

Think historically about how people have reacted to change. It can cause great upheavals in society, with violent reactions while other changes brought through various experiences are welcomed and may change how people live and comprehend the world. Experiences affect us emotionally in many cases rather than logically and when we respond emotionally, behaviours become unpredictable. This causes the paradoxes, anomalies and inconsistencies mentioned in the rubric. If we were logical beings the world would be an easier place, but probably more boring.

These definitions all point to the fact that memory is the key to experience. The experience is stored in memory and drawn upon when the circumstances are repeated or closely mimicked so we can deal with them — hopefully better than on the initial experience.

Experiences can come in many ways and the synonyms listed below for experience help us to understand the concept even further. They assist in defining how an experience can arise:

Synonyms

actions	understanding	judgment
background	wisdom	observation
contacts	acquaintances	perspicacity
involvement	actuality	practicality
know-how	caution	proofs
maturity	combat	savoir-faire
participation	doings	seasonings
patience	empiricism	sophistication
practice	evidence	strife
reality	existences	trials
sense	exposures	worldliness
skill	familiarity	forebearance
struggle	intimacy	
training	inwardness	

http://www.thesaurus.com/browse/experience?s=t

These synonyms show partly the vast array of words that our language has created around this concept, and also shows how important it is in the human psyche. We, as humans, want to experience. Now we will look at some examples of experiences and examine how they can have an impact. It is also important to remember that experiences do not have to be positive. You might experience a huge problem, a bereavement, a car accident, an unwelcome relationship or something totally bizarre that rocks your world. There can be a more opaque side to any experience that may need to be addressed.

The whole aim of this Common Module is to examine the text closely but also relate it to the concept of human experiences and decide how examining it in this way enables us to better understand both the text and the concept of humanity.

It is important that you unpack what each text you study shows you about human experiences and what ideas / themes arise from those experiences. Formulate your own ideas about the text.

Read the NESA Stage 6 document called *English Stage 6: Annotations of selected texts prescribed for the Higher School Certificate 2019-23* (see *www.educationstandards.nsw.edu.au*) for the set text you are studying. This document offers insights into the way each particular text should be examined by outlining key ideas and areas for clarification.

Human experiences and ways of experiencing vary due to individual circumstance and these experiences can change many things about individual lives, communities and the world. When we examine the concept of human experience in relation to a text, we need to examine the assumptions or biases we bring to it as well as how experiencing the text itself may change us and how we view things. The text may challenge and confront how we view the human experience or we may have preconceived ideas that make it more difficult for this to happen.

Students can also think about their own 'personal experience to make connections between themselves, the world of the text and their wider world.' Examining and enjoying any text is an experience in itself but it is what we take away from the text and apply that is the crucial aspect. That is not to say that every text will be enjoyed or offer a human experience that is significant either positively or negatively. Some texts may not personally engage you and that is fine. This is especially so when you begin to look for other related material that links to *Texts and Human Experiences*. We recommend that you find examples of texts that link but also personally appeal to you so that you can relate empathetically with them.

Individual Human Experiences

The idea of personal experiences is a popular and pervasive concept, especially in the literature of many cultures. Recording personal experiences as a means of sharing wisdom or more mundane daily tasks is part of human nature and we record and relate these experiences frequently. Experiences are recorded and relayed in many ways. We tell oral stories in both anecdotal and formal ways, we write, draw, sing and photograph our way into history (or not). Look at the proliferation of social media in this current century as people record their daily, even hourly, experiences for all to see. We record the most trivial details of our lives for likes and followers while the real world passes us by. Human experiences affect us on a daily basis and some experiences influence our lives and the way we live them.

Individuals seek out experiences in a variety of ways. Some seek more and more extreme experiences to test themselves against the world. Others limit their experiences. A lot of people prefer the familiar and don't actively seek new experiences. Individuals, it must be remembered, also see experiences in different ways and the same experience may have a very different impact on individuals. The one thing we can be certain about is that experiences are part of humanity and even the most limited of us have them. Many of these experiences also come from interaction with others and as noted we also like to share these experiences.

Experiences are what define us in many ways and are what makes us human.

We are going to look at four specific ways that experiences can influence us as people over the next few pages. These are physical, psychological, emotional and intellectual experiences and many experiences are a combination of these.

Physical Experience

The concept of a physical experience is tied into the human experience and part of the collective experience as well. Individuals seek physical experiences to test themselves against nature and other individuals often as part of trials and rituals, for example being integrated into a community. In modern times individuals have sought to test themselves with extreme sports and explorations into the harshest conditions and even space. Physical experiences can also change the way we see the world and others because of the chemical changes these experiences have on our bodies and mind. Physical experiences are often challenges and part of the experience is overcoming adversity. These physical challenges are often celebrated, as in the case of sports, but can also offer challenges if the experience is a negative one such as an accident or disease. Physical experiences are also often quite public and thus have permeated our societies in both their execution and how they are perceived. These physical experiences, even if experienced vicariously, have become popular across cultures and celebrated. Think of examples for yourself but most competitive sports offer examples.

Bruce Lee extends the concept of the physical experience into all aspects of life and that's what we will look at next in our analysis of human experiences –

'If you always put limits on everything you do, physical or anything else, it will spread into your work and into your life. There are no limits. There are only plateaus, and you must not stay there, you must go beyond them.'

Psychological Experience

The idea of a psychological experience is tied into many of the abstract ideas that people experience and can lead to a discussion of what is normal psychology. From the earliest times humans have attempted to alter their psychology through a number of experiences. On a simple level this can be a drug that changes the person's or group's perspective on reality. Examples of this might be alcohol or marijuana but cultural groups also use various substances to share group experiences. This can be seen in Native American cultures with *peyote*. In more modern times prescription drugs that are mood altering have been used to minimise the symptoms of psychiatric illnesses such as depression, and these mood altering drugs are common and legal. Others attempt to alter their psychology by seeing specialists in this area while others act out their condition leading to social and criminal issues. When discussing the human experience, psychology is a key issue and will form a part of most studies of experience. When taken too far this search for a new psychological experience can be harmful eg. an addiction.

Carl Jung, the famous psychologist, comments on the problems of addiction for human experiences, stating clearly that excess can be an issue:

"Every form of addiction is bad, no matter whether the narcotic be alcohol, morphine or idealism."

Emotional Experience

According to the psychologist, Robert Plutchik, there are eight basic emotions:

- **Fear** — feeling afraid.
- **Anger** — feeling angry. A stronger word for anger is rage.
- **Sadness** — feeling sad. Other words are sorrow, grief (a stronger feeling, for example when someone has died) or **depression** (feeling sad for a long time without any external cause). Some people think depression is a different emotion.
- **Joy** — feeling happy. Other words are happiness, gladness.
- **Disgust** — feeling something is wrong or nasty
- **Trust** — a positive emotion; admiration is stronger; **acceptance** is weaker
- **Anticipation** — in the sense of looking forward positively to something which is going to happen. **Expectation** is more neutral; **dread** is more negative.

https://simple.wikipedia.org/wiki/List_of_emotions

Emotions are the strongest drivers of human experience and form lasting aspects of any experience. Think about breaking up with someone you love and the emotions that drive behaviours in this situation. People have all sorts of extreme behaviours under the influence of emotions and these experiences are often the ones recorded and those which influence us most. Think about the role emotions play in our lives and the range of emotions from the list above. Consider how much emotions affect our life experiences, how they influence our decisions which decide our experiences and on a higher level consider how they affect the decisions which may seriously impact our experiences, such as politicians going to war.

Intellectual Experience

The concept of an intellectual experience is linked to decisions and experiences we have based on analysis and logic rather than the emotional choices referred to in the previous section. These intellectual experiences have changed the way we live and how we have seen our world. These experiences have affected the way we as humans have altered our world to suit our needs and lead to all the great advances in human society and thus experiences. Changes in our ideas, beliefs etc. alter the way we interact with the world and often these intellectual changes come at great cost.

Think of the time in Europe when the Church dominated and stopped scientific advances by calling them heresy/witchcraft. Open societies are more open to new ideas and this is what has hastened the pace of intellectual experiences as dominant ideologies fall away. Intellectual advances may not have the excitement that the other types produce but perhaps they have a more lasting impact on people, societies and the world in general. Ideas are powerful experiences and people hold beliefs strongly.

Immanuel Kant stated that:

"experience without theory is blind, but theory without experience is mere intellectual play."

Consider this statement in the light of what we have learnt about human experiences. Are they a combination of many factors or can we isolate experiences into simple forms?

What exactly is a human experience?

The titular question reminds us of the old brainteaser: "If a tree falls in a forest and no one is around to hear it, does it make a sound?"

There are two classic responses to this. The more Platonically-minded would say the tree always makes a sound when it falls in the forest. We don't have to be there to hear it; we can imagine the sound of a tree falling in the forest, based on memory of such an event or on the recording of such an event. We know that sound is just vibrating air, and it's safe to say that air always vibrates in response to a tree falling, or a bear growling, or a cicada singing, whether we are there to hear it or not.

The second answer is a more post-structuralist response: the sound doesn't occur on its own; it needs a human ear to be heard. Therefore, if there is no human in the forest to hear the tree fall, then there is no sound. This automatically implies that "experience" of anything requires the presence of a human being, which means there is no such thing as an experience that *isn't* human.

Animal rights activists – or anyone with a beloved pet – would almost certainly reject this notion because it prioritises humans and relegates all other species to a lower class of being: an attitude that most would agree has gotten the human race into an awful lot of environmental trouble over the last 200 years of industrialisation.

In his article (*What is an Experience?*), my learned colleague Paul Hartley describes experience in its most basic form, as "the perception of something else" and "ultimately information about what we have perceived." But does this make it particularly human? Dogs and cats perceive things. Insects perceive things. You could even say that plants perceive things, such as the direction from which the sun is shining. Perception is the most basic of life's survival tools for all manner of flora and fauna.

In her brief but cogent disquisition on the subject (*What is Human?*), another of my learned colleagues, Nadine Hare, asserts that to be human is a social construct. Hartley builds on that notion by suggesting that culture affects experience when we start to share it, because "the words, associations, and priorities we attach to the shared experience define how we understand the world we live in."

Hare rightly points out that this world is increasingly dominated by consumerism, which has distorted what it means to be human by excluding all of the attributes and qualities that "make people people." Calling us consumers reduces our experiences to mere transactions. It defines human experience within the narrow confines of the purchase funnel and has little interest in anything that isn't a purchase driver.

Perhaps the field of commerce is where the experiential rubber most emphatically meets the road. Unlike mere perception, commerce is a uniquely human experience. It has mediated, automated, and dominated the human agenda to the point where we are defined by what we buy and little else. Commerce has invaded the non-profit spheres of government, health, and education, imposing its own priorities and principles on these institutions in the expectation that they will behave more like businesses. And even though business still strives to appeal to the so-called masses, it prioritises the pursuit of individual wealth, and in so doing, not only inhibits the desire for shared experience but unravels the social fabric historically woven by the democratic tradition.

As if in response, that social fabric is being re-woven by our networks. As Hare asserts, "humans both produce technology and are produced through technology." Experience is shared more now than it ever has been because the experiential platform – i.e., that very human invention called the internet – is in place to facilitate it like never before, and on a global scale.

This sharing capability reintroduces all of those things that "make people people" back into the conversation – whether commercial or political. What "makes people people" is messy, unpredictable, emotional, and complex. Most of what makes us human has no place in the experiential confines of the purchase funnel, and defies any of our attempts to place it there.

The challenge for us as a species is to embrace this new capacity for sharing to keep the agendas of our hegemonic institutions – whether commercial or political – from defining what makes an experience human. A post-consumer business strategy might be one that, as Hare hopes, will "expand our view of people to include the complex and dynamic social, cultural, gendered, spiritual and racialised beings that they are." Maybe then will our shared human experience truly become, as Hartley asserts, the glue that holds us all together as human beings.

Will Novosedlik
MISC magazine

https://miscmagazine.com/what-is-a-human-experience/

This article appeared in the September 2014 edition of MISC magazine. Can you relate to what the article says about human experiences? Do human experiences depend on perception? Does the experience of anything require the presence of a human as experiencer (para 3)? Can the ideas of experience be extended to include perception by plants or animals? Hartley's idea is that "shared human experience" is "the glue that holds us all together as human beings". Is this an oversimplification?

The Impact of Human Experiences

Human experiences have impacts on many levels. On an individual level, we can have changes in our assumptions about the world and people around us; we can ingest new ideas and have these open new vistas of productivity and performance. We can also reflect and build on these experiences to ensure that they are even more meaningful to our lives. Behaviours towards others and the way we respond to the world can manifest themselves in new and different responses. An example might be that through adverse experiences we can build resilience so that the next negative experience isn't as traumatic and we accept it for what it is. Experiences also teach us new behaviours on a very physical level — if you burn yourself once on a flame you learn not to do it again (hopefully).

The impact of human experiences can also be shared in groups and societies. Firstly, let's examine some group dynamics that can be affected by human experiences. Groups share experiences and adapt and develop behaviours that impact on the group as a whole. Think about the notorious 'bonding' sessions sporting teams have that unite them in a common goal. Think about the behaviours of various gangs in our society. We see plenty of examples of this on American television where gangs based on ethnicity and social groupings form specific sets of behaviours that impact on how they interact with each other and the world. These groupings carry assumptions about how they see the world and respond to it. For example, they may have generally negative reactions to law enforcement and this is ingrained into their codes of behaviour. They are suspicious of the world and the people in it — dividing them up into threats, the law and victims. These behaviours are often reinforced by group experiences such as the initiation rituals which are integral to membership.

Often the impact of these behaviours is to perpetuate stereotypes that then categorise the individuals within these groups. The graphic I have included here shows a stereotypical gang member with the suspicious gaze, ubiquitous hoody and scruffy look. These stereotypes reject new ideas and maintain assumptions about the world, often to the detriment of their members. The experiences they have reinforce their own stereotypical way of viewing anything outside the safety of the group and the cycle continues. Of course, other groups have more positive impacts and see the world as a very different place and their experiences are designed to be positive interactions. Think about groups such as Rotary who are constructive in the community. Other groups have specialty interests such as Animal Welfare, Surf Lifesaving and charities.

Normal social interactions impact groups and individuals, but it takes a major event to alter the behaviours of whole societies, especially so in the modern world where societies are large in scale. Earlier in human history smaller experiences could alter the behaviour of societies as they were insignificant in size compared to modern ones. We often fail to remember that many of these ancient societies' behaviours were impacted by superstition, religions and cultural habituation. The modern society as we know it is only a recent phenomenon. Just a few hundred years ago with church rule people were forced to think in a specific

way and punished for not adhering to a theological culture. Think of the Spanish Inquisition, the imprisonment of Galileo and other such restrictions on freedom of thought; scientific breakthroughs were hidden or declared witchcraft. Even recently the world has seen societies kept repressed by failed ideologies. The brutality of such regimes has left deep scars on the social psyche of nations as they try to recover. This has had an impact on the human experiences of whole populations, and societies respond accordingly.

One example might be at the conclusion of the Communist regime in East Germany when the Berlin Wall was destroyed as a visual symbol of the new-found freedom of a whole population of people who had been repressed for decades by a brutal and ever-present regime. Many citizens who had grown up in this system, where you could 'disappear' without trial or real evidence, found the idea that you could express yourself incredible. Many of the

East Germans couldn't believe that this freedom was real and that the Stasi (the secret police) were gone.

Other experiences can affect societies in extreme ways. Think about wars and the impact they have on civilian populations.

Climatic events such as earthquakes change the way that people behave and respond to situations. Catastrophic flooding occurred in the US city of New Orleans in 2005. The US President's response to help was not immediate and the national administration was severely criticised for lack of effective action.

Societies also respond to perceived problems such as pollution. In 1989 the oil tanker Exxon Valdez ran aground in Prince William Sound, Alaska with disastrous results. The effects of this event are still being experienced thirty years later.

Societies can be divided, as we saw with the election of Donald Trump in the United States of America and the reaction of the Political Left.

The impact of human experiences on societies can be quite dramatic, as we have seen, while other experiences (such as an election) can go by without a murmur from societies, no matter who wins. As a last thought before we move on you should also consider the impact of the media on societies in the modern world, and how they influence individuals, societies and the development of ideas.

Problems With Human Behaviour

So far, we have discussed the impact of human experiences on behaviour. Now we can begin to develop some more complex judgements and understandings about the impact of those experiences on human behaviours. In simplistic terms it could be assessed as:

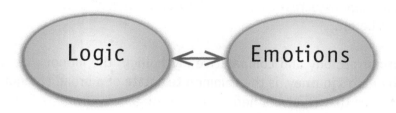

These two opposites on the continuum certainly shape the manner in which we see incidents and how they affect the experience. For instance, if someone you love has no interest in you, it creates a very different reaction to someone you don't care about having no interest in you. It is generally agreed that humans respond more strongly with emotion than they do with logic. Often, it is only through time and reflection that we can understand how an experience has changed and/or altered the manner in which we see a situation or individual.

The Role of Storytelling in Human Experiences

Storytelling has been part of the human experience since 'people' began communicating and it is a method used to convey information and experience as well as be entertaining. Earliest myths were all oral and then people began to write down stories so they weren't lost in time. From this, various theories have developed around storytelling and one is the 'monomyth', which is a template across cultures for storytelling. Let's have a look at this below.

'In narratology and comparative mythology, the monomyth, or the hero's journey, is the common template of a broad category of tales that involve a hero who goes on an adventure, and in a decisive crisis wins a victory, and then comes home changed or transformed.

The concept was introduced in *The Hero with a Thousand Faces* (1949) by Joseph Campbell, who described the basic narrative pattern as follows:

"A hero ventures forth from the world of common day into a region of supernatural wonder: fabulous forces are there encountered and a decisive victory is won: the hero comes back from this mysterious adventure with the power to bestow boons on his fellow man."

Campbell and other scholars, such as Erich Neumann, describe narratives of Gautama Buddha, Moses, and Christ in terms of the monomyth. Critics argue that the concept is too broad or general to be of much use in comparative mythology. Others say that the hero's journey is only a part of the monomyth; the other part is a sort of different form, or colour, of the hero's journey.

https://en.wikipedia.org/wiki/Hero%27s_journey

Storytelling in History and its Purpose in Human Experience

Storytelling in oral form was accompanied by some theatrics to make the stories as entertaining as possible. Many of the early narratives were based upon religious ceremonies and stories of the creation of the earth and people(s). As time moved on, these stories were accompanied by dance, music and/or theatre and often were part of lengthy rituals, often taking days. These stories were designed to bring meaning to people's lives by explaining their own existence and the purpose/meaning of life in a time when life expectancy was short and entertainment was scarce. Of course stories were also recorded as these experiences were significant to all people and these stories run across all cultures. Before writing, stories were recorded in pictures such as cave art, in tattoo designs on skin and in designs such as rock piles and the giant carved heads of Easter Island.

Writing changed the manner in which stories were told and many of the old oral traditions were lost, barely being kept alive by specialists. Stories began to travel across cultural and national boundaries on whatever surface could be created. Papyrus, bones, pottery, skins, paper and in more modern times film, video and digital storage have changed, over time, the way in which stories of human experience have been told and shared. Content evolved from myth, fable and legend to history, personal narratives and commentary. Modern narrative form often has an educational or didactic element and can drift into propaganda. Stories of self-revelation can be instructive and give audiences the opportunity to apply learning to individual lives, whereas historically narrative was used in this way for societies and groups as a whole. In recent times narratives have become interactive and audiences can choose how the narrative unfolds.

Whatever form the story takes we all have a seemingly innate need for narratives to make sense of our lives. They either confirm our world view or alter our world view depending on the experience they convey and the experiences that we bring to the narrative. We need to remember that narratives are important to human experience and have been significant since the beginning of time.

The Text as an Experience

The concept of the text as an experience is one area to consider as we look at *Texts and Human Experiences*. Reading or viewing the text is an experience in itself and when we do this we bring our own history (experiences) to the text and this helps shape our understanding.

Think about the personal perspective that you bring to a text. What are some of your experiences that might influence how you read a particular text? Some texts, especially personal narratives of trial and tribulation or loss, can be confronting to some audiences and bring back strong opinions or emotions. Many texts attempt to do this as they convey a particular point of view about the world.

Does what you bring to the text affect what you learn from that text? We also need to delve into how the narrative experience is conveyed and how this in turn impacts upon the manner in which the story is received by audiences across different cultures. For example, Western films where heroes fight Islamic terrorism may well be viewed very differently by audiences in Western democracies and Islamic countries. Even seemingly innocuous narratives like the movie 'The Red Pill' which is about men's rights and created by a woman, has caused a polarisation of views wherever it has been shown. Strong personal experiences and viewpoints certainly bring their own understandings to texts.

Questions for Texts and Human Experiences

- Define the module in your own words.
- How are people connected by shared experiences?
- How might physical experience(s) change the way you respond to the world?
- How do you think a person's context and prior experiences shape how they perceive the world?
- Are experiences unique or do prior experiences have an impact on a current experience and way of seeing life?
- What is positive about human experiences?
- Discuss what is negative about human experiences.
- To what extent does experience shape the way we see other people and / or groups?
- Is an individual's culture part of their experience or is it something else?
- Is it possible not to have any meaningful experiences at all?
- Why do people tell stories?
- What do you think you might learn from a narrative?

STUDYING A DRAMA TEXT

The medium of any text is very important. If a text is a drama this must not be forgotten. Plays are not *read* they are *viewed*. This means you should never refer to the "reader" but the "audience" as the respondent to the text. The marker will want to know you are aware of the text as a play and that you have considered its effect in performance. Shakespeare will occasionally give explicit instructions on how the scene is to be performed and how the actors are to respond to the language he has chosen to use, but as we will see later little stage direction overall. Remembering a drama text is a play also means when you are exploring *how* the composer represents his/her ideas you MUST discuss dramatic techniques. This applies to any response you do using a drama, irrespective of the form the response is required to be in.

Dramatic techniques are all the devices the playwright uses to represent his or her ideas. They are the elements of a drama that are manipulated by playwrights and directors to make any drama effective on stage! You might also see them referred to as dramatic devices or theatrical techniques.

Every play uses dramatic techniques differently. Some playwrights are very specific about how they want their play performed on stage. Others like Shakespeare give virtually no directions as we have discussed. They might give detailed comments at the beginning of the play and/or during the script. These are usually in italics and are called *stage directions*. They are never spoken but provide a guide to the director and actors about how the play is to appear and sound when performed.

Some common dramatic techniques are shown on the diagram that follows.

DRAMATIC TECHNIQUES

Setting – *the set, what style is it and why?*

Character costuming: *does it change as the play progresses? How is colour, style and texture used?*

Lighting: *how is shadow and illumination used to represent ideas?*

Stage type – *what effect does this have on the impact of the messages?*

Character gestures and mannerisms: *how does what characters do represent their personality and thematic purpose?*

Symbols and motifs: *how is repetition of image/idea used to maximise the play's effect?*

DRAMATIC TECHNIQUES

Sound: *Music and sound effects. Why are these chosen and how are they delivered?*

Stage blocking and movement: *Where do characters position themselves on stage and how do they move?*

Line delivery – *tone, pace, volume, pausing, intonation…*

Conflict: *the action, Man vs man, Man vs nature, and/or Man vs himself*

Special Effects: *This broad category especially refers to technical devices used for effect. Eg. slide shows, motorised movements, hologram effects etc… Why are these used?*

SHAKESPEARE THE DRAMATIST

A BRIEF BIOGRAPHY

Shakespeare was born at Stratford-upon-Avon on April 23 1564. While he was baptised two days later there is not a lot of documented evidence on his life. His father was a glover and leather merchant who later went on to the position of Alderman in the town. Mary, his mother, was a landed heiress so it is thought that Shakespeare's early life was quite comfortable.

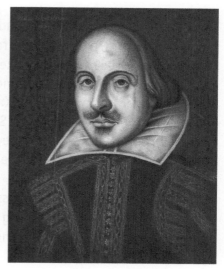

Little is known about his early years but it is assumed that he had an education at the local grammar school. He was married at eighteen to Anne Hathaway who was pregnant. She was eight years older than him and they eventually had three children. In the late 1570s his family began to have money problems and he seems to disappear for several years. He resurfaces in London around 1588-92. There are several unsubstantiated rumours as to his whereabouts during this time including fleeing from poaching problems, school teaching and acting.

It is assumed that Shakespeare began acting in Richard Burbage's company and he began to make his mark writing with the *Henry VI* plays. In 1593 the plague struck London and the theatres were closed. He began to write long poems such as 'The Rape of

Lucrece' and his sonnets. By 1594 the theatres opened again and the players had a new patron, the Lord Chamberlain. Shakespeare had become a shareholder in the company and began to produce two plays a year.

By 1598 he was quite wealthy and able to afford to buy a large house in Stratford, a coat of arms for the family and formal status for himself (i.e. the right to be called a gentleman). In 1603 Queen Elizabeth died and James I became King. The players were given a Royal Charter and became the King's Men. Shakespeare walked in James' coronation procession. Shakespeare at this time began to write his great tragedies between 1604 and 1608. In 1608 his company took over Blackfriars Theatre, a good winter venue.

His company was the most successful in London and he became successful in his own right, being quite famous and popular. He began to slow down in his work and plan for retirement. He died, aged 52, on 23rd of April, 1616.

Shakespeare's works were published after his death by two friends, John Heminges and Henry Condell, in the First Folio editions. He leaves us a vast body of work and even in death he left a rhyming curse on his tomb.

> 'Good friend, for Jesus' sake forbeare
> To dig the dust enclosed here.
> Blessed be the man that spares these stones,
> And cursed be he that moves my bones'.

SHAKESPEARE'S LIFE AT A GLANCE

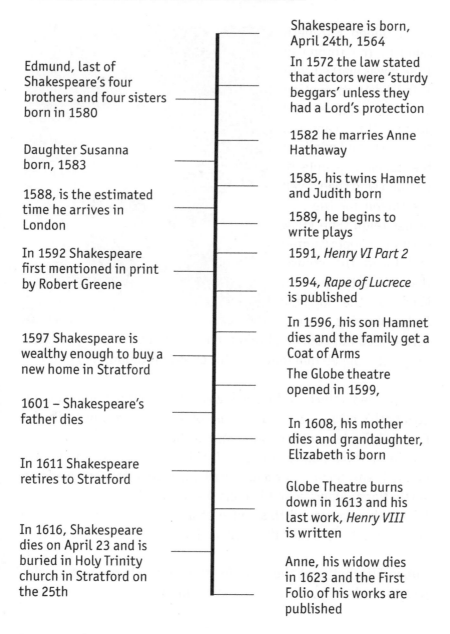

Shakespeare is born, April 24th, 1564

Edmund, last of Shakespeare's four brothers and four sisters born in 1580

In 1572 the law stated that actors were 'sturdy beggars' unless they had a Lord's protection

Daughter Susanna born, 1583

1582 he marries Anne Hathaway

1585, his twins Hamnet and Judith born

1588, is the estimated time he arrives in London

1589, he begins to write plays

In 1592 Shakespeare first mentioned in print by Robert Greene

1591, *Henry VI Part 2*

1594, *Rape of Lucrece* is published

In 1596, his son Hamnet dies and the family get a Coat of Arms

1597 Shakespeare is wealthy enough to buy a new home in Stratford

The Globe theatre opened in 1599,

1601 – Shakespeare's father dies

In 1608, his mother dies and grandaughter, Elizabeth is born

In 1611 Shakespeare retires to Stratford

Globe Theatre burns down in 1613 and his last work, *Henry VIII* is written

In 1616, Shakespeare dies on April 23 and is buried in Holy Trinity church in Stratford on the 25th

Anne, his widow dies in 1623 and the First Folio of his works are published

SHAKESPEARE AND THE ELIZABETHAN ERA

When Queen Elizabeth came to the throne in 1588 it was marked with a four day coronation of extravagance and pomp. This captured the hearts and minds of the common people of England who then loved the Queen for the rest of her reign. She knew what her people wanted and loved the crowds that came to see her. Much of the intrigue and plotting which surrounded her court and reign did not affect the everyday man unless it stopped him following his chosen religion.

Life was generally hard for the lower classes but generally Queen Elizabeth's reign is seen as a time of wealth and prosperity for England. Trade to other countries was begun or improved as the sea became England's domain. The trade route to Russia was opened, the Spanish Armada crushed, attempts were made to settle North America and Francis Drake sailed around the world. Elizabeth encouraged this sense of adventure, which began to spill into other parts of life such as the arts.

Queen Elizabeth set the tone for the court where much of this wealth ended up. She was stylish, intelligent and demanded the same from those around her such as the Maids of Honour who needed to have accomplishments such as languages, musicianship, dance and horsemanship to stay in court. Dress was important and this was helped by the import of starch into England during her reign. It was used to keep all those clothes stiff, especially those huge ruffs they wore.

Her dress during this period was complicated layers and the ladies of the court copied this style. It took ages to dress and help was required to put on all the layers of clothing. The men's clothes were also stiff and uncomfortable. The children copied the parents' clothes, the little girls even having corsets to pull the body into shape. Of course this dress did not extend to the lower classes whose clothes were far more suitable for general living and working. Their clothes were more flexible and loose fitting with broad brimmed hats and solid boots fit for work.

Country living was mainly about farming and feeding a growing population, as England was expanding. The farmer paid rent to the landlord and most followed an open field system. During the Elizabethan years farming was profitable and a class of wealthy farmer called yeomen did well for themselves. Prosperity improved lifestyles and houses were more solidly constructed.

While little schooling was offered in the country the wealthy could send their children to schools in the town. Wealth also gave people more leisure time and this was often spent around church activities. Despite the power of the church, the supernatural played a role in everyday life and many still believed in its powers. While villages still burnt the occasional witch much 'healing' was done at the village level.

Town life could be hard for the large numbers of vagrants or 'work shy' and they became a problem. Elizabeth set laws that sent these men to work in workhouses or on farms. City living conditions were poor and with no sanitation, rats and narrow streets, many places were smelly and diseased. London was the most important town and the 'city' was the centre of business and government. Elizabeth rarely travelled outside of the city areas and never saw parts of the country she ruled.

The growing wealth and prosperity of the times was seen in the growth of the theatres, one of the most popular forms of entertainment. Before the growth of theatres, plays were held at inns. Food and drink were sold to the audience during the performance and there was often riotous behaviour. In 1570 the Mayor of London banned theatre performances in the city so the theatres moved to the edges. As time went on the Puritan influences declined and the theatre became more respectable and a company called the Queen's Men was formed meaning that they had her approval. James Stuart, King after Elizabeth, enjoyed the theatre and so they became the King's Men and were led by Shakespeare.

People of all classes still believed in the Divine Right of Kings. This Divine Right said that the ruler was God's representative in the world and any change would result in chaos in the kingdom. This is why the penalty for treason was death as it was a direct act against God. Also, there was belief in the Great Chain of Being. God was at the top and everything else in classes below him. It was carefully ordered with the King at the top of worldly order followed by the church, princes, nobles and common man. All animal and plants were below man. It was thought any upset in the order would result in chaos.

Elizabethan England is generally described as a time of prosperity, peace at home and quarrels abroad. This sense of peace and prosperity led to improved lives and a more educated populace. The people had time to pursue new ideas as they moved away from the old medieval way of thinking about all things. With great exploits in travel and new ideas many people had opportunities that would not have been possible before. This was part of the Elizabethan legacy.

ELIZABETHAN ENGLAND AT A GLANCE

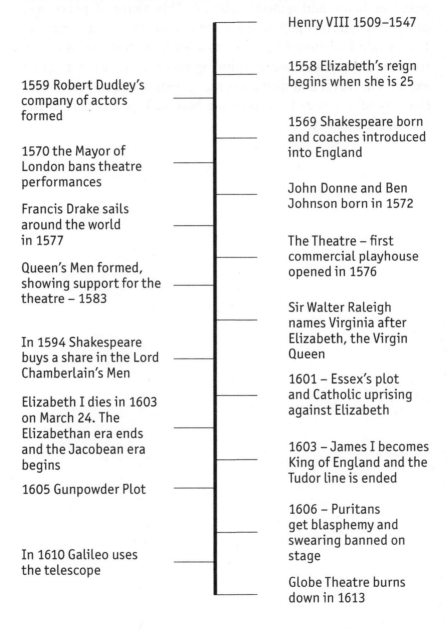

Henry VIII 1509–1547

1558 Elizabeth's reign begins when she is 25

1559 Robert Dudley's company of actors formed

1569 Shakespeare born and coaches introduced into England

1570 the Mayor of London bans theatre performances

John Donne and Ben Johnson born in 1572

Francis Drake sails around the world in 1577

The Theatre – first commercial playhouse opened in 1576

Queen's Men formed, showing support for the theatre – 1583

Sir Walter Raleigh names Virginia after Elizabeth, the Virgin Queen

In 1594 Shakespeare buys a share in the Lord Chamberlain's Men

1601 – Essex's plot and Catholic uprising against Elizabeth

Elizabeth I dies in 1603 on March 24. The Elizabethan era ends and the Jacobean era begins

1603 – James I becomes King of England and the Tudor line is ended

1605 Gunpowder Plot

1606 – Puritans get blasphemy and swearing banned on stage

In 1610 Galileo uses the telescope

Globe Theatre burns down in 1613

PLOT OUTLINE

Antonio laments the fact that he is so melancholy. His companions Salarino and Solanio try to work out why.

The Princes of Morocco and Arragon pick the wrong caskets.

Antonio's friend Bassanio tells him that he needs money to woo the beautiful Portia.

Meanwhile Shylock's daughter Jessica plans to elope with Lorenzo, a Christian.

Antonio suggests that he be guarantor for the loan.

Jessica and Lorenzo set off to Belmont, taking Shylock's money and jewels.

Bassanio leaves with Gratiano, to seek Portia's hand.

Shylock, the Jew, agrees to lend Bassanio the money.

Shylock is angered that Jessica has left and stolen his money.

The bond for the money will be a pound of Antonio's flesh.

Bassanio and Portia fall in love. Luckily, he chooses the correct casket and wins her hand

Portia and Nerissa discuss the inadequacies of the suitors for Portia's hand.

News comes that Antonio's ships have all been lost at sea.

Portia's father's will decrees that whoever chooses the casket with the portrait of Portia in it can marry her.

Shylock demands the forfeit in the bond.

Gratiano and Nerissa declare their love, as Lorenzo and Jessica arrive.

A letter tells Bassanio that Antonio is ruined and Shylock intends to take Antonio's pound of flesh. Bassanio immediately returns to Venice.

Portia and Nerissa follow, disguised as young men.

Portia enters the court as Balthasar. She pleads that Shylock show mercy to Antonio.

She also offers him three times the loan, but Shylock demands the pound of flesh.

Portia agrees that the law allows Shylock the flesh and asks Antonio to prepare himself.

Just as Shylock is about to cut Antonio's chest, Portia points out that the bond allows only for flesh, no blood.

Shylock realises that he is defeated, so he offers to take the money.

Portia will not allow this, adding Shylock must forfeit property.

Antonio also insists that he convert to Christianity.

Shylock leaves, a broken man.

Still disguised, Portia and Nerissa talk Bassanio and Gratiano into giving them their rings.

Back in Belmont, dressed as themselves, Portia and Nerissa demand the rings and tease the men for giving them away.

Eventually they tell the men about the disguises, and return the rings.

The three couples are happy as the play ends.

PLOT SUMMARY AND ANALYSIS

ACT 1 SCENE 1 – VENICE

Here we meet Antonio, who *is* the merchant of Venice. He imports goods by sea. He reports that he is in an unhappy frame of mind, though he does not know why. His friends Salarino and Solanio suggest that Antonio is worried about his business investments, as he has three ships currently at sea, loaded with cargo. Antonio rejects this suggestion. He also rejects Solanio's declaration that he must be in love.

Bassanio (an Italian lord) enters, with Lorenzo and Gratiano. Salarino and Solanio leave.

Antonio tells them that he regards the world as 'A stage where every man must play his part, / And mine a sad one.' (line 88-9) Gratiano tries to make him laugh, but fails. He and Lorenzo leave.

Bassanio tells Antonio that he wishes to court the beautiful and rich Portia of Belmont, but that he needs to borrow some money from Antonio to do so. (He has borrowed money from Antonio before and not yet paid it back.) He says that he has seen in her eyes that she is interested in him, but that she has many suitors. Antonio says that all his money is tied up in his cargo ships at the moment, but he gives Bassanio permission to borrow money, using Antonio's name as surety.

Act 1 Scene 1 Commentary

This scene introduces the audience to two of the play's main characters – Antonio and Bassanio. Antonio is confident in the strength and security of his business matters, but nonetheless finds himself in a depressed state of mind, over what he does not know. Still, he is most willing to help out his friend Bassanio in his courting of Portia, even though Bassanio already owes him money and all of Antonio's wealth is currently at sea. Bassanio might strike the audience as rather immature and not really a good friend, if he already owes Antonio money and is now asking him to go into debt so that Bassanio can chase a woman. Antonio's generosity might seem even reckless: 'be assured / My purse, my person, my extremest means / Lie all unlocked to your occasions.' (line 136-8). So, Antonio is prepared to risk a great deal for his friend. Modern productions have sometimes seen a suggestion of homosexuality in this. Perhaps Antonio's melancholy *is* because he is in love – with Bassanio. This says much about the humanity and good nature of Antonio.

Shakespeare's audience would have recognised this scene as reinforcing their pre-existing ideas about Italians, especially Venetians. It is a culture of affluent young men, basically hanging around, chatting, going to dinner and so on. As well, they are prepared to run considerable risk in pursuit of a beautiful woman. This play works on the stereotypes of the period to reinforce the ideas and this is another aspect of human experiences.

As the scene ends, the audience would recognise that Antonio is entering into something potentially dangerous in giving permission to his friend to seek a loan with Antonio as guarantor. The other thing this scene does is it introduces the subject of marriage, and the object, in this case – the rich and beautiful Portia, whom we are about to meet in Scene 2.

ACT 1 SCENE 2 – BELMONT

Portia and her waiting woman Nerrissa discuss the various suitors that have come seeking her hand in marriage. They put them all down, for various reasons, except for Bassanio. Portia says: 'I remember him well, and remember him worthy of thy praise.' (line 98)

During the conversation we learn that Portia's father has died and that in his will he has determined that suitors to Portia's hand must undergo a test in which they choose between a gold, a silver and a lead casket. In one of these caskets there is a portrait of Portia. He who finds the portrait, gets Portia, with all her wealth, as his wife. Suitors who fail the test must swear never to marry anyone else. So far, no one has taken the risk involved in making a choice. Portia expresses her desire to choose her own husband in her own way, but she must obey her late father's wishes.

Anyway, Portia and Nerissa have quite a bit of fun, and the audience with them, in their derogatory descriptions of all the suitors, except Bassanio. They are really a set of cultural stereotypes, used for the purpose of humour. For example, the Scottish suitor is a big drinker, the French suitor isn't very manly and the Neopolitan (southern Italian) one only ever talks about his horse. The Elizabethan audience would have recognised and been amused by, these stereotypes.

As the scene ends, a serving man announces the imminent arrival of a new suitor—the Prince of Morocco. Portia does not sound pleased.

Act 1 Scene 2 Commentary

This scene is very amusing, as Portia and Nerissa mock the qualities of the various suitors who want to marry Portia. The audience will note that they come from a wide variety of cultures and places, and that Bassanio is the only one who is northern Italian, as Portia is. So, the one she likes best is also the one most like her in race, culture and place of origin. This is reinforced by her reaction to the coming of the Prince of Morocco: 'the complexion of a devil' is a reference to the Prince's dark skin.

This scene can be a simple, delightful one as two young women survey and poke fun at the qualities of Portia's various suitors. On the other hand, if you want to, you can play it as a little more sinister. Portia can be portrayed here as conceited, valuing herself very highly. She can even be seen as racist, especially in what she says about the Prince of Morocco. This is a more modern interpretation as the context has changed over time.

This is the audience's 'first impression' of Portia, one of the play's central characters, so it is important that she convey the impression that we want the audience to carry with them throughout the play.

ACT 1 SCENE 3 – VENICE

Bassanio has found someone to lend him three thousand ducats, for three months — the Jewish usurer (money-lender) Shylock. Shylock asks to speak to Antonio, and, in an aside, he says that he hates Antonio because he is a Christian, he lends money without interest and he has publicly expressed anti-Jew sentiments and anti-usury sentiments in the past. 'Cursed be my tribe / If I forgive him.' (line 43)

Antonio arrives and Shylock greets him with false warmth. Antonio says that he doesn't usually lend or borrow. Shylock tells a Biblical story about the lending of sheep for interest, but Antonio responds that 'The devil can site scripture for his purpose.'

Shylock responds that Antonio has called him a 'misbeliever' and a 'cut-throat dog', but for 'these courtesies' (sarcasm) he'll now lend him the money he needs. Antonio says that he'll probably insult him and spit on him again. Shylock then offers to lend the money without interest, but if the loan is forfeited he will cut out a pound of Antonio's flesh, from whatever part of his body he chooses. Shylock refers to this arrangement as 'a merry sport', just a joke really.

Bassanio opposes this idea, but Antonio accepts saying that he expects to receive many times more than 3,000 ducats within the next three months, when his boats return.

Shylock leaves as Antonio mocks him, saying: 'The Hebrew will turn Christian, he grows kind', suggesting that only Christians will do kind acts. Bassanio refers to Shylock as a villain.

Act 1 Scene 3 Commentary

The dislike that Antonio and Shylock feel for each other is palpable in this scene. It is based on ancient grudges and prejudices held by Christians against Jews and vice-versa.

Modern productions have sought to make Shylock a sympathetic character. Certainly, Antonio has treated him badly in the past, calling him 'misbeliever', 'dog' and spitting at him, and he even says that he intends to do so again in the future. Against this background, it is not surprising that Shylock hates Antonio and might relish having him at an advantage in the contract for the pound of flesh. Antonio claims that the real reason Shylock hates him is because Antonio lends money without interest, thus taking business away from Shylock.

How do we want the audience to react to the contract? Is it barbaric and less than human for Shylock to propose it, or is it a matter for Antonio, that he is foolish to accept it? Nothing can shake Antonio's confidence in his ships coming in, making him a fortune.

ACT 2 SCENE 1 – BELMONT

The stage directions call the Prince of Morocco a 'tawny Moor', a reference to his race and the colour of his skin, which is 'tawny' brown rather than black.

The Prince begins by appealing to Portia (and probably to the audience as well) that he not be judged by the colour of his skin, which is the result of exposure to the 'burnished sun'. The highest regarded virgins from his part of the world have loved his skin and he doesn't want to change it. Portia explains that, due to her father's will, it isn't her choice anyway: 'Besides, the lottery of my destiny / Bars me the right of voluntary choosing.' (line 15) She says, therefore, that the Prince has as much chance as any other, and is, in that sense, as 'fair' as any who has come for her hand.

The Prince asks to be led to the caskets. Portia reminds him that if he chooses wrongly, he must agree to never marry anyone. He concedes this and she leads him to dinner, saying that he will choose the casket after. He says that fortune is going to either bless him or curse him.

Act 2 Scene 1 Commentary

Casting of the Prince of Morocco will have a significant effect on the nature of this scene. If he is cast as older, overweight, ugly, then Portia will be laughing at him (with the audience) when she says threat he has as much chance as any suitor. If we cast him as young tall and handsome, then Portia might be genuinely attracted, and flirtatious towards him. Productions of *The Merchant of Venice* have surrendered to cultural, and even racist, stereotypes in this scene in their depiction of the Prince of Morocco. You can use this point to relate to human experiences especially in terms of assumptions and emotional responses.

ACT 2 SCENE 2 - VENICE

Lancelot Gobbo, the clown, struggles with his conscience in trying to decide whether to leave the employ of Shylock the Jew. He refers to Shylock as 'the very devil incarnation'. (line 20)

His near-blind father, Old Gobbo, comes along, and, failing to recognise his son, he asks for directions to Shylock's house so that he may find Lancelot. Lancelot gives him confusing directions and then plays a trick on him, telling him that his son has died. Finally, Lancelot reveals the deception to his father and convinces Old Gobbo that he is in fact Lancelot. He tells his father that he is leaving Shylock in the hopes of working for Bassanio.

Just then, Bassanio arrives. Lancelot and Old Gobbo, in their bumbling way, ask Bassanio to take Lancelot on as his employee, and Bassanio agrees (once he figures out what they are talking about.) He sends them off to resign from Shylock. Gratiano arrives prevailing upon Bassanio to allow him to accompany him to Belmont to see Portia, promising to curb his wild behaviour. They agree that his behaviour will, nonetheless, be appropriate for tonight as they celebrate Bassanio's departure for Belmont.

Act 2 Scene 2 Commentary

Lancelot would have been played by Will Kemp, the resident clown of The Kings' Men and Shakespeare's favoured comic actor at the time. The humour in the first part of this scene is based on the idea of Lancelot having an argument with himself as one part of him, 'the fiend', tells him to leave Shylock while his conscience tells him to stay. It is as though he is the central figure in a morality play, with a fiend and his conscience pulling him in opposite directions. This provides the actor with opportunities for physical comedy.

When Old Gobbo arrives, the humour is mainly on the old man who is easily duped because his eyesight is so poor. Lancelot includes the audience in this by speaking an aside which tells the audience that he and the old man are son and father. When Bassanio comes, the humour comes from the jumbled attempts of the Gobbos to get Bassanio to take Lancelot with him as a servant. As they leave, the audience is expectant of future comic scenes involving the Gobbos. The audience is also promised an evening of 'merriment' with Bassanio and Gratiano.

ACT 2 SCENE 3 – VENICE

Shylock's daughter Jessica, bids farewell to Lancelot, saying that she will miss him because he made the household cheery when it is otherwise 'hell'. She asks him to secretly deliver a letter to Lorenzo, one of Bassanio's friends. Lancelot leaves, offering the observation that he'll be surprised if some Christian doesn't marry her, because she is so beautiful.

In a short soliloquy, Jessica regrets the fact that she is 'ashamed to be my father's child!' (line 16) She expresses the hope that Lorenzo will keep his promise and make her 'a Christian and thy loving wife.' (line 20)

Act 2 Scene 3 Commentary

Here love is now pitted against being Jewish, and becoming Christian is a step up for a Jew. Lancelot implies that Jessica's extreme beauty might make her lucky enough to be courted by a Christian. His remark also assumes that she would accept. The situation of a daughter wanting to marry someone her father doesn't like is a staple of theatre and film, but here it has a racial basis. At least it is being conceded that a Jewish woman can be beautiful! Think about the human experiences we are seeing here, individual motivations, prejudices and ways of seeing the world that Shakespeare represents.

ACT 2 SCENE 4 – VENICE

Lorenzo, Gratiano, Salarino and Solanio are gathered. Lorenzo proposes that they separate to put on disguises for the masque carnival and meet in an hour at his lodgings.

Lancelot arrives, giving Lorenzo the letter from Jessica. Lancelot says that he is going to Shylock's house to invite him to dine with Bassanio. Lorenzo tells Lancelot to secretly convey the message to Jessica that he will not fail her. He then confides in Gratiano that he intends to take Jessica from her father's house.

Act 2 scene 4 Commentary

Tension is building as an evening of masked merriment approaches. The Elizabethan audience would have had an expectation of revelry and humour, but also amusing misunderstandings, in the context of the masque. As well, we wonder what will come of Bassanio's invitation to Shylock to dine. Also, we understand that Jessica's plan to run away with Lorenzo is fraught with danger.

ACT 2 SCENE 5 – VENICE

Shylock, with Lancelot, calls on Jessica. When she arrives, he tells her he is invited to dinner. He says that he is invited in hate and he doesn't want to go, but that he will anyway. He asks her to look after the house, and gives her his keys. He says there is some ill brewing because he dreamt of money bags last night and this is a bad omen.

Lancelot tells him that a masque is planned, and this sends Shylock into another rant, telling Jessica not to even stick her head out the window to get a look at 'Christian fools with varnished faces'. (line 31) He tells her to 'Let not the sound of shallow foppery enter / My sober house.' (line 34) In other words, he doesn't want even the sound of the festivities to enter his house or influence his daughter.

Lancelot goes ahead of Shylock and tells Jessica that she should look out of her window for a Christian coming by. Of course he means Lorenzo. Jessica lies to Shylock, telling him that Lancelot merely said '"Farewell mistress", nothing else.' (line 43) When Shylock goes, Jessica says 'goodbye' to him, saying that if things go as she hopes, he has lost a daughter and she a father. Think here about the strong emotions that motivate Jessica and the way that 'love' has changed the way she sees her future.

Act 2 Scene 5 Commentary

Shylock is something of a kill-joy, no doubt, and he doesn't seem to relish a party. He is concerned about his possessions and the fact that he had a dream that boded badly. But, these are fairly common characteristics of middle-aged men in Shakespeare, especially in relation to protecting their daughters from the dangers of the world and members of the opposite sex.

These qualities could make Shylock sympathetic. We know that he is well-intentioned, and we also know that he will fail to keep his daughter under lock and key, as he would like.

ACT 2 SCENE 6 - VENICE

Gratiano and Salarino, in masks, wait for Lorenzo. Gratiano speaks of the pleasure of the chase. Lorenzo arrives, saying that he had affairs to deal with, causing him to be late.

He takes them to Shylock's house and Jessica appears ('above, in boy's clothes') probably in a window. Lorenzo and Jessica exchange declarations of love, then she expresses her embarrassment at being dressed as a boy. He asks her to come down and be his torch bearer, but she objects that being a torch bearer will make her too easily seen when she should hide. He assures her that in her disguise she will not be discovered. She says she will secure the doors, grab some ducats and be down straight away.

Gratiano makes a joke that Jessica is 'a gentle and no Jew'. (line 52) By 'gentle' he means well-bred, but it is also a pun on 'gentile' (non Jew). Jessica re-appears on the street and they set off to the masque.

Antonio arrives with the news that Bassanio sails to Belmont immediately, so Gratiano had better forget the masque and hurry along. Gratiano says he is glad about it.

Act 2 Scene 6 Commentary

Jessica and Lorenzo conduct a delightful little love scene, she is in boy's clothes and speaking from a window. The existence of their relationship suggests racial integration in Venice, not conflict. All of Lorenzo's friends seem accepting of the relationship, though it has been noted that they don't speak to her.

Antonio's appearance at the end of this scene makes it clear to the audience that he cannot have been involved in Jessica's disappearance.

ACT 2 SCENE 7 – BELMONT

We return to Belmont where the Prince of Morocco has dined and is ready to make his choice of caskets in an attempt to marry Portia. Portia tells him that the 'winning' casket contains a picture of her.

He finds that each casket has an inscription: the gold one says: 'Who chooseth me will gain what many men desire', the silver one: 'Who chooseth me will get as much as he deserves' and the lead one says: 'Who chooseth me must give and hazard all he hath'. He makes a long speech considering the pros and cons of each, ultimately deciding on gold. Portia gives him the gold key and he opens the casket. He says 'O hell! What have we here?'

Inside he finds a 'death's head' skull with some lines of verse that begin 'All that glisters is not gold'. The Prince says: 'Cold indeed, and labour lost' and 'thus losers part' (line 77) as he goes.

Portia responds with 'A gentle riddance'. (line 78)

Act 2 Scene 7 Commentary

Shakespeare builds the tension leading to the first attempt at picking the casket for Portia's hand by having the Prince of Morocco speak an extremely long speech articulating his thought processes leading to the decision to open the gold casket.

If the audience has been laughing at the Prince all along, then it will take Portia's 'gentle riddance' to mean 'good riddance'. If we cast the Prince as a handsome, winning young man, then we will feel more sympathy for him and Portia's remark could be said with an amount of regret. Having said that, the Prince is most commonly played as an unattractive man with way too high an opinion of himself, and it is a relief when he chooses the wrong casket.

ACT 2 SCENE 8 – VENICE

Salarino and Salanio recount what they have seen. Bassanio and Gratiano have set sail and Lorenzo is *not* with them. Shylock had raised the alarm with the Duke who went to check Bassanio's ship to see if Jessica and Lorenzo were on it, but the ship had already set sail.

The Duke is told that Lorenzo and Jessica were seen on a gondola. Antonio certifies that Lorenzo and Jessica were not on the ship.

Solanio does an impersonation of Shylock crying in the street: 'My daughter! O my ducats! O my daughter!' (line 15) 'Justice! Find the girl! / She hath the stones (jewels) upon her and the ducats!' (line 22)

Salarino changes the tone by recalling an encounter he had with a Frenchman who said that a Venetian ship had gone down. Salarino hopes that it was not one of Antonio's. He goes on to say what affection Antonio has for Bassanio and how he told Bassanio to concentrate on his love for Portia and not to worry about the bond with Shylock. He saw Antonio's eyes fill with tears as he shook Bassanio's hand.

Solanio says: 'I think he loves the world for him' (Bassanio). He proposes that they go to Antonio and try to cheer him up. Salarino agrees.

Act 2 Scene 8 Commentary

Solanio refers to Shylock as 'The villain Jew' and 'the dog Jew' during this scene. He also mocks Shylock's distress when he finds out that Jessica has cleared off and taken his money and his jewels. This speech will no doubt be accompanied by facial and hand gestures to add to the humour. The implication, of course, is that Shylock is much more upset about losing his ducats and jewels than he is about losing his daughter.

This is another of the scenes where some have seen evidence of 'gay' relationships, especially in Antonio's feelings toward Bassanio. Salarino's description of Antonio holding back tears as he shakes Bassanio's hand goodbye and wishes him well in his pursuit of Portia, can be accounted for with the idea that Antonio is in love with Bassanio. The alternative view is that what we are seeing is the intensity of true male friendship, Venetian style. Whatever you think the intensity of human experiences is strong in this scene.

ACT 2 SCENE 9 - BELMONT

This time it is the Prince of Arragon (in Spain) who has come to choose a casket and hopefully win Portia's hand in marriage.

He rejects the gold because it says 'Who chooseth me, shall gain what many men desire' and he reasons that he is not a man that follows others, that goes along with the crowd. He likes the silver one because he reasons that he will get what he deserves.

Consequently he is quite offended when he finds that what is inside the silver casket is a portrait of an idiot and a poem telling him that he is a fool. Still, he accepts the rules of the game and leaves quickly.

Next, a messenger brings news that a young Venetian has arrived (presumably Gratiano), announcing the approach of his lord (Bassanio) who wishes to try his luck with the caskets. He describes Gratiano as a likely ambassador of love.

Portia says to Nerissa that they should quickly go and see who it is, and Nerissa hopes that it is Bassanio.

Act 2 Scene 9 Commentary

Another verbose and self-absorbed suitor chooses the wrong casket. You might notice that the reasons of both the Princes of Morocco and Arragon for choosing as they did were essentially related to their over-assessment of themselves. The audience, of course, is 'cheering' for Bassanio and so are happy to be rid of the other two, as Portia is as well.

Shakespeare teases the audience by having us hear of Bassanio's approach and see the excited anticipation of Portia and Nerissa, only to have the scene cut there. We must wait to see what happens next.

ACT 3 SCENE 1 – VENICE

Salarino tells Solanio that he has heard that another of Antonio's ships may have been ruined.

Shylock arrives, still talking about his daughter's rebellion. They ask him if he knows whether Antonio has lost any ships at sea. Shylock replies that Antonio should 'look to his bond'. Salarino doubts that Shylock would enforce the bond. 'What's that good for?' (line 41) he asks. Shylock's reply is one of deep bitterness, as he says it will feed his revenge as Antonio has interfered with his business, laughed at his failures, mocked his successes and scorned his nation. The reason, he says, is because he is a Jew. Shylock then asks a series of rhetorical questions, aimed at making the point that Jews are like everyone else – human. He also points out that Christian's, in their treatment of Jews, have taught Jews how to take revenge, so he will do so to Antonio. It is intriguing here that we get to see Shylock's interpretation of his human experience and that he too sees himself as 'human' first and foremost despite others seeing his role as a Jew and moneylender first.

A servingman of Antonio's comes to fetch Salarino and Solanio to Antonio's house. They go, as the Jew Tubal arrives.

Shylock bewails the loss of the jewels and Jessica. He says that he wishes to see her dead, with the jewels and ducats in her coffin. He says there are no sighs but his and no tears but his.

Tubal tries to comfort Shylock by pointing out that others have troubles too, for example Antonio losing his ships. Shylock jumps at this as good news, thanking God and saying 'good news, good news!' (line 83)

Tubal then tortures Shylock with stories he has heard about the speed with which Jessica is spending the money and that she exchanged a turquoise ring, with sentimental value to Shylock as it was given to him by 'Leah', for a monkey!

Act 3 Scene 1 Commentary

This is a very important scene, because some of the central ideas in the play are expressed. Shylock warns that he *will* in fact take his bond (the pound of flesh) from Antonio and that he will do it out of revenge. He tells them that Antonio has mistreated him in the past, wholly and solely because he is a Jew.

What follows is one of Shakespeare's most famous speeches and a significant one for our study of human experiences in this text. It is an appeal for tolerance between races on the basis of common humanity – Shylock argues that Jews are the same as everyone else. He does so, by asking a series of rhetorical questions. (These are questions asked for effect. In this case they have an 'implied answer' of 'yes'.) 'Hath not a Jew eyes? Hath not a Jew hands, organs, dimensions, senses, affections, passions?' (line 46) If we answer 'yes', then why should we regard Jews as different? Shylock continues, coming to his telling conclusion: 'If you prick us, do we not bleed? If you tickle us, do we not laugh? If you poison us, do we not die? And if you wrong us, shall we not revenge?' (lines 50–52)

This argument brings Shylock to his dreadful point – Jews will take revenge, just like everyone else. In fact, Christians, by their treatment of Jews, have *taught* Jews about revenge. What he means is that Christians have taken perpetual revenge on Jews ever since the crucifixion of Christ by Jews. He is saying that the prejudice and hatred of Jews is an act of revenge by Christians against Jews for killing Jesus Christ. Therefore, the Christians, having taught Jews all about revenge, will understand if a Jew takes his revenge on a Christian. Therefore, Shylock will do what no one expected him to – he will have his pound of Antonio's flesh.

You may have heard the expression 'to have your pound of flesh'. It has entered the language as a way of describing the situation where someone demands what is due to him, even if it hurts someone else. In the play it is literal, because they really are talking about a pound of flesh on Antonio's body. In general usage it could be used to refer to any kind of debt or revenge.

Shylock's argument for tolerance is a powerful one. It is one of the memorable things in this play. It might make us think that, although some of the characters in the play are racists, the play itself is not. You need to think about how this fits into the specific ideas on human experiences and how different cultural assumptions impact on the experiences the characters undergo.

There are a lot of things to consider in this. Shylock is a dislikeable character, for reasons other than the mere fact that he is Jewish.

He is a strict father who seems to have lost his daughter's affection. He does seem to care more about his money than his daughter. He seems to have no personal relationships at all, everything is business. It is apparently his intention to take a knife and cut out a pound of flesh from the body of a living man. This is a 'fairly' extreme thing for anyone to do, in any context. If you think that these are negative character traits that are unique to Shylock, then that's one thing. If, on the other hand, you think these characteristics are being presented as typical of all Jews, then that's racism.

There again, it could be that Shylock's Jewish characteristics are the product of long-term racist attitudes and behaviours that Jews have been subjected to. If you and your family had been treated as evil, called 'dog', spat on in the street and so on, for generations, mightn't you take revenge if the opportunity arose? Is it surprising that Shylock would have a chip on his shoulder?

There is also no doubt that Shylock is being driven by his embarrassment and loss over Jessica's elopement. Not only has she disobeyed and robbed him, but with a Christian, making it worse. She will be lost to the family, but lost to the 'nation' as well.

What about Antonio? Everyone else in the play speaks of him as though he's a saint, yet he has abused Shylock and says he would do so again. And what if we do play him as gay? Where does that leave us – two minority groups (Jews and gays) coming into conflict? Salarino and Solanio are essentially comic characters, but should we laugh at their racist remarks? Can we expect a modern audience to accept that characters such as Antonio, Solanio and Gratiano can be likeable and racists at the same time?

These questions are for each production of the play to sort out. As well, you, in developing your own view of the play and human experiences, need to think these things through. What would you do if you were directing a production of *The Merchant of Venice*, today?

Producing and directing a play is a matter of balance. Every decision you make, especially casting, will have an effect on everything else about the play.

ACT 3 SCENE 2 – BELMONT

Portia, Bassanio, Gratiano, Nerissa and all their trains (presumably quite an impressive gathering) are on stage. Portia clearly wants Bassanio for her husband, but modesty prevents her from saying so openly, though she does put to him that he delay choosing the casket, in case he chooses wrongly and is thereby forced to leave. But Bassanio is anxious to make Portia his wife, so he proceeds, finally choosing the leaden casket, which does contain the portrait of Portia. His reasoning to choose the lead one shows his superiority to the other two previous suitors as he speaks on the subject of the difference between outward appearance and inner value. He chooses the lead because its outer plainness suggests an inner beauty, which is what he finds.

The rhyme in the casket instructs him to kiss Portia, but he requests her permission first. This is very gentlemanly of him, as he has already won her according to her father's device. She declares herself and her possessions to be his, and gives him a ring which she asks that he never remove. He agrees, saying he will die before he removes the ring.

Gratiano and Nerissa also announce their love, proposing a double marriage. Next Lorenzo and Jessica arrive, Gratiano referring to them as 'Lorenzo and his infidel'. They are accompanied by a messenger called Salerio. He has a letter from Antonio to Bassanio saying that Antonio is financially ruined and that Shylock is demanding his pound of flesh. He asks that he may see Bassanio one more time before he dies. Bassanio is filled with guilt, having been enjoying an ideal existence with Portia while his friend, who financed the whole thing, is ruined and in mortal danger. He explains to Portia that he is less than nothing, being in debt. Portia offers to pay Shylock two or three times the debt, but both Jessica and Salerio warn that Shylock wants revenge more than money.

Portia proposes that they marry immediately then Bassanio and Gratiano leave for Venice to sort the matter out. She expresses confidence that Antonio will dine with them soon.

Act 3 Scene 2 Commentary

Portia is a woman of high birth, and she has obligations in regard to her father's will, therefore she cannot be too blunt in her expression of affection for Bassanio. She is prepared to urge him not to choose for another month or two, so that she has his company, but when he tries to get her to use the word 'love', she will not. Presumably, that would be being too open about her feelings. Nevertheless, she makes it clear that she wants him to succeed with the caskets, by her language and the rising anxiety of her speech, line 39-62, which ends by saying that it is more difficult for her to watch what happens than for him who is participating in it.

Note how different her manner and tone is from when she was dealing with Morocco and Arragon, the suitors she did not like. With them she was confident and sarcastic, while here she is coy and sweet. Shakespeare here gives us a clear insight into human behaviour and the anomalies and inconsistencies in it according to circumstance.

Just the same, the effect of this whole passage will depend a lot, in the theatre, on the positioning of Bassanio and Portia, in regard to each other. Think of how different it will be if they are in each other's arms at the start of the scene than if they are on opposite sides of the stage, speaking to each other from a distance. Or maybe they are together at centre stage, but not actually touching. That kind of positioning will bring emphasis to their, as yet, unconsummated passion.

Bassiano's speech about outer and inner beauty is a set piece on one of Shakespeare's perennial themes – appearance and reality. The gold appears valuable but contains nothing, but the lead appears nothing and contains the great prize. This speech reflects very positively on Bassanio's judgement, especially in regard to his choice of Portia. Unless the audience thinks that there is 'magic' in Portia's father's test, and Bassanio chooses *correctly* because he is the *correct* suitor.

Whether Portia is another example of 'good on the outside, bad on the inside' has been a question throughout the play so far. She is beautiful and rich (good on the outside), but is she also spoilt, vain and superior (bad on the inside)? A lot will depend on how we have 'played' her in the scenes with Morocco and Arragon. Was she unnecessarily cruel, or did they deserve it anyway? The audience's impressions of this will depend on how we have cast and played Portia and the two Princes.

It would be possible to summarise the action of the choosing very briefly, but Shakespeare, again, spins it out in order to manipulate tension in the audience, building up to the climax of the correct choice of the lead casket.

Gratiano's use of the word 'infidel' to describe Jessica might get a reaction in the theatre today that is different from the one it would have got in Elizabethan England. An infidel is someone who does not believe what you believe. So, a Jew is an infidel to a Christian because Jews don't believe in the divinity of Jesus Christ. Today, we hear the word in the context of being used by Muslims to refer to non-Muslims — Westerners, Christians, Jews, anyone who does not believe what Muslims believe. It has a very emotive connotation because it is sometimes used in an aggressive context, in relation to Islamic jihad, the idea of a 'holy war'. It is interesting to note how things change, isn't it? In Shakespeare's play, he is using the word 'infidel' simply to mean what it says, *probably* without any connotations. Gratiano is Lorenzo's friend, and he should not intend to speak ill of Jessica, who is Lorenzo's beloved. In fact, it is interesting to note that nobody in the play ever speaks to, or about, Lorenzo suggesting that he shouldn't fall in love with a Jew. Critics have, though, noted that none of the others actually speaks to Jessica, which could reflect some attitude to her or tension about having her present.

The Venetians see love as being above all those considerations. Just the same, you might consider whether the word 'infidel', in the first decade of the 21st century, in Australia, has taken on meanings that Shakespeare did not intend and might be best replaced with something else. This, would, of course be self-censorship and undesirable – some would say a crime in itself. Would it be a consideration in a production for *your* local community?

At line 302, Portia says 'First go with me to church and call me wife / And then away to Venice to your friend!' After Bassanio reads the letter from Antonio, she says 'Dispatch all business and be gone.' (line 320) I am assuming that they do marry, along with Gratiano and Nerissa before they leave for Venice. Nothing more is said about marriage, but their behaviour toward each other subsequently, would surely suggest that they do marry before Bassanio and Gratiano leave for Venice to the court. In Act 3 Scene 4 both Portia and Lorenzo refer to Bassanio as Portia's husband and Gratiano as Nerissa's husband.

I can't let 'Solerio' pass without some comment. Shakespeare has two characters in Venice called 'Salarino' and 'Solanio'. As if that isn't confusing enough, in this scene he has a messenger arrive called 'Solerio'. Many editors have assumed that 'Solerio' must be an accidental misspelling of 'Solanio' or that it is a transposing error. Remember that these were all done by hand, printing errors were common and that 'er' could readily look like 'an' in scribbled handwriting. Anyway, the editor of your prescribed New Cambridge edition of the play believes that as we can't prove that an error occurred, we must proceed with three characters named Salarino, Solanio and Solerio. Mercifully, Solerio only appears in Act 3 Scene 2, and briefly in Act 4 Scene 1, so you can forget about him after that.

ACT 3 SCENE 3 – VENICE

The Jailer has brought Antonio to Shylock to plead with him. Shylock will not listen, saying: 'I'll have my bond...Thou call'dst me dog before thou had'st a cause / But since I am dog, beware my fangs.' (lines 4–7)

Solanio calls Shylock an 'impenetrable cur' (line 18) (A dog that you can't have any effect on.) Antonio gives up, saying that the Duke will have no choice but to enforce the bond and that he hopes that Bassanio will come back to see him die. Otherwise, he doesn't care.

Act 3 Scene 3 Commentary

This scene reinforces what Jessica and Solerio predicted about Shylock's desire for revenge. He repeats the argument that if you call someone 'dog', then don't be surprised if they behave like one. He again accuses Antonio of abuse and prejudice against Shylock before he had reason. Antonio responds by saying that the real reason Shylock hates him is because he has helped Shylock's debtors pay their debts rather than forfeit to Shylock. So, Shylock is saying that it is about bigotry whereas Antonio is saying it is about money.

The audience can't really tell what is the truth here. Antonio's explanation fits in with Shylock's other behaviour and with Jewish stereotypes. Shylock's explanation is believable and much more sympathetic. A lot will depend, as always, on how we play Shylock. If he is being calm and 'business-like' we might more readily believe Antonio's story. But if Shylock is more passionate, obsessive and irrational, then we might believe he is driven by generations of resentment and prejudice, that he wants to punish

Antonio as a representative of all Christians. They could, of course, both be right.

ACT 3 SCENE 4 – BELMONT

Lorenzo compliments Portia on her ability to bear the absence of Bassanio. Portia says that Antonio, being Bassanio's 'lover' (we would say 'close friend'), she assumes he must be like Bassanio. She tells Lorenzo that she and Nerissa are going to stay at a near-by monastery until the return of their husbands. She leaves Lorenzo and Jessica in charge of her house.

She sends her servant Balthasar to Padua with a letter to her cousin Dr Bellario. Balthasar should bring whatever Dr Bellario gives to him to Venice to meet Portia, who will already be there.

She tells Nerissa that they will soon see their husbands, but that they won't be recognised because they will be done up as young men. Portia has in mind many ways of convincing others that she is male. She says that her coach is waiting for them at the gate, and that they have a twenty-mile trip ahead of them.

Act 3 Scene 4 Commentary

Here, Portia takes control of the situation. She tells Lorenzo and Jessica that she and Nerissa are going to stay at the monastery as a kind of retreat until their husbands return, but the letter to her cousin Dr Bellario and the talk of dressing as young men, lets the audience know that her real plans are elsewhere. The fact that they will see their husbands tells the audience that they are going to Venice, but at the end of the scene we don't know why. This leaves the audience in a state of expectation and curiosity.

One thing we do know is that Portia is a capable and determined young woman and that she has decided that it is time for her to 'take over'.

ACT 3 SCENE 5 – BELMONT

This scene begins with comic banter between the clown Lancelot and Jessica. Lancelot makes a pun on the word 'bastard', telling Jessica that her only hope of salvation would be if she wasn't really Shylock's daughter (making her a bastard, born out of wedlock.) Jessica says that she has been saved by her husband (Lorenzo) because he has made her a Christian. Lancelot objects to him having done so on the grounds that it will increase the price of pork. (This would be because Jews don't eat pork, but the more Jews convert to Christianity, the more pork eaters there will be, so the price will go up, due to demand.)

Lorenzo arrives, telling Lancelot that 'the Moor' is pregnant with his child. This is maybe a reference to a black slave left by the Prince of Morocco, who is now pregnant by Lancelot. (There is no other mention of 'the Moor' in the play.) Lancelot eventually leaves to see to that the preparation of dinner is coming along.

Lorenzo asks Jessica her opinion of Portia. She replies that she might make Bassanio so happy that he will find all 'the joys of heaven here on earth'. (line 64) Lorenzo claims that he is just as good a husband as Jessica says Portia is a wife, but Jessica says they will discuss it over dinner, when she can 'digest' things. She makes a pun on 'digest', as they will be eating.

Act 3 Scene 5 Commentary

This is a comic interlude to keep the audience waiting for what Portia has planned in Venice. It tells us that Lorenzo and Jessica are happy and secure in each other's love, but little else.

Some of the humour is based on race, so you need to decide how you would present it. As well, as my recounting of it above shows, the jokes may need a lot of explaining for a modern audience to understand them, thereby destroying any humour that they may have been in the first place.

If you left this scene out, or reduced its length substantially, nothing much would be lost. It tells the audience that all is well in Belmont, while the action is shifting to Venice. In terms of human experiences it suggests that Shakespeare knows that his audience requires some humour and a break in the tension in the theatrical experience.

ACT 4 SCENE 1 – VENICE, THE COURT

The Duke, judges (Magnificoes), Antonio, Salerio, Gratiano and others enter. The Duke warns Antonio, almost as if he is apologising, that he is going to have to answer to 'an inhuman retch, / Uncapable of pity' (line 5), Shylock. Antonio replies that he is 'armed / To suffer with a quietness of spirit / The very tyranny and rage of his.' (lines 11–13). Thus Antonio is to be seen as noble, extremely brave and stoic, while Shylock is further slandered as something less than human.

Shylock enters and the Duke instructs that he face him. He tells Shylock that he (and everyone else) thinks that Shylock has no real intention to carry out this bond against Antonio, but is leaving it to the last minute so that his mercy will shine out, making him seem like a better person. Shylock replies simply that he demands his bond, otherwise Venetian law will be a mockery. What he means is that it is vital to Venetian law and order that bonds be enforceable. If this bond can be broken, then any bond can.

He says that if you ask why he has decided to enforce the bond, to have a weight of flesh rather than 3,000 ducats, it is because it is 'my humour'. (line 42) Here Shylock toys with them, saying something along the lines that he wants the pound of flesh because he feels like it. But he does concede to the existence in him of 'a lodged hate and a certain loathing / I bear Antonio'. (line 60)

Antonio appeals to the others that they not bother to try to reason with Shylock, but just let him have his way.

Bassanio offers Shylock double the money owed to him but Shylock refuses. He goes on to compare the example of the bought slaves that the Venetians have working in their homes. He says that Venetians treat them like animals because they own them. He says that he owns the pound of flesh in the same way, having paid for it in the same way as they have for their slaves. He says that if he tried to tell them how to treat their slaves, they'd tell him that they have the right to treat them any way they like. Similarly, he has the right to do what he likes with the pound of Antonio's flesh.

Antonio tries to satisfy Bassanio's anguish, saying 'I am a tainted wether of the flock', / Meetest for death' (line 114), meaning that he is the one who is worthy to die, rather than Bassanio. Gratiano slings insults at Shylock, such as 'thou damned inexecrable dog'. (line 127) Shylock's reply is that 'I stand here for law'. (line 142)

Suddenly Nerissa arrives, disguised as a young man. She hands the Duke a letter from Bellario, which the Duke reads aloud. It says that Bellario's opinion of the case will be represented by a young 'doctor' from Rome, called Balthasar. The Duke extends a greeting to Portia (Balthasar) showing her (him) a place to stand in the court. Portia asks which is the Jew and which Antonio, and is told.

She begins by conceding that Venetian law cannot prevent Shylock from having his bond. Then, she says: 'Then must the Jew be merciful.' (line 178) Shylock is defiant, asking why is it that he *must* be merciful.

What follows (lines 180-202) is Portia's renowned set piece on mercy. It is eloquent, high minded and based on Christian values. She says that mercy is 'twice blest' because it blesses the giver and the receiver. We all want mercy, therefore we should all give it. How does the concept of mercy fit into your understanding of the human experience in the text?

Shylock's response is a cold one: 'I crave the law, The penalty and forfeit of my bond.' Bassanio calls on the Duke to do something that is a little wrong (deny Shylock's suit) in order to do something that is a larger good (save Antonio's life). But Portia contradicts him, saying that there is no power in Venice that can alter a contract. It will become a legal precedent and many wrong decisions will follow on. Shylock praises this 'wise, young judge'. (line 220)

Portia appeals to him again to take three times the money, but he will not listen, so she tells Antonio to prepare his bosom for the knife. She calls for a surgeon to assist in stopping the bleeding, but Shylock will not allow this either, saying that he cannot find it written in the contract.

Antonio is called upon to speak his last. He says: 'I am armed and well prepared.' (line 260) He asks Bassanio to tell his wife (Portia) that Antonio loved him. He says that he will pay the debt instantly with his heart, if Shylock cuts too deep.

Shylock prepares himself to cut into Antonio's chest, when suddenly Portia changes tack: 'Tarry a little, there is something else.' She points out that the bond does not allow Shylock to take any blood. Not only that, but if he does shed any blood his property can be confiscated by the state.

Gratiano mocks Shylock's previous enthusiasm for 'Balthasar': 'O upright judge! / Mark, Jew – O learned judge!' (lines 308–9)

Portia says, in a threat, 'Thou shall have justice more than thou desirest.' (line 312) She is turning Shylock's own insistence on the letter of the law into a weapon against him. Shylock quickly backs down and agrees to take the three times monetary reimbursement, and Bassanio agrees. But Portia stops him, saying that Shylock *must* cut Antonio's flesh. But if he takes any blood or takes too much flesh, he will be sentenced to death and all his property confiscated.

Shylock says he'll take just the money he is owed, and again Bassanio agrees, but Portia is still not satisfied. She says that in Venetian law it says that if an alien seeks the life of a citizen, then the citizen may have half the alien's possessions, the state the other half and the life of the alien is at the mercy of the duke. Finally, she calls on Shylock to get down on his knees and beg the Duke for his life.

The Duke immediately pardons Shylock's life, in order to demonstrate how different he is from Shylock who would not show mercy. Shylock says: 'You take my life / When you do take the means whereby I live.' (line 372) Shylock feels that his work *is* his life.

Antonio suggests that only one half of Shylock's goods be taken and held until Shylock's death at which time it will be inherited by Lorenzo, as Jessica's husband and Shylock must give all of the possessions he retains to Jessica as well. In return, Shylock must become a Christian.

Shylock's reply is simply: 'I am content.' (line 389) He goes.

The Duke instructs Antonio to reward Portia (Balthasar) in some way as he owes her (him) so much. The Duke leaves. Portia says that the satisfaction of the outcome is enough reward. But when Bassanio presses her further, she asks him for the ring that he had been given by Portia and promised never to take off. Eventually, after many arguments by Bassanio to put her off, she leaves without the ring. But Bassanio is pressured by Antonio and he decides to give Portia the ring. He sends Gratiano to run after them with it.

Act 4 Scene 1 Commentary

This scene contains the central action of the play, and it is also the scene for which the play is principally remembered as it captures much about the human experience.

Theatrically it is tense and exciting, and quite ghoulish. The tension in the audience builds, as Shylock, wielding a sharp and glittering knife, moves closer and closer to the moment when he cuts into Antonio's chest. Shakespeare, having placed this image into the minds of the audience, takes them to the very brink of the mutilation, before Portia, who appears to be on Shylock's side, finally stops things with the line 'Tarry a little, there is something else.'

What Portia has been doing is allowing Shylock to dig himself in deeper, by insisting that the letter of the law must be carried out. She then uses this principal against Shylock by explaining that the letter of the law is that he must cut one pound of flesh exactly and no blood at all. Of course, this is impossible.

Worse for Shylock, if he fails to comply, he will forfeit his property to the state and can even be sentenced to death. For Portia has a further piece of law that if an *alien* (a Jew, for example) threatens the life of a *citizen* (Antonio), then half the alien's property can be seized by the citizen.

In just a few moments, Shylock is reduced to being on his knees, begging the Duke for his life. The Duke is a decent enough person to immediately grant Shylock his life, though he does point out that he is showing mercy to Shylock who would not show mercy to Antonio.

We might wonder about mercy, though, in relation to Portia. The very fact that such a law exists is an example of the treatment meted out to Jews in Venice. They cannot be citizens and must always wear the label of 'aliens', outsiders, strangers, minorities – choose what you will.

At some point during all this, the audience may feel that Shylock has been punished enough. I can tell you that *this* audience member usually feels that way *long* before his punishment is ended. I do realise that this is a man who says he wants to cut a pound of flesh out of another man's chest, but Shylock is still human (see Act 3 Scene 1 'Hath not a Jew eyes?' and so on) and he must have *some* rights, surely. I might be a sentimental fool, but when I read or watch the play, I'm happy when Portia points out that he can't spill any blood and Bassanio offers to give him the money back. In fact, to me, it looks like everyone is happy about this except....Portia.

Why does Portia drive on so relentlessly with the revenge against Shylock? Why can't she show him some of the mercy that she herself described so eloquently only a short time before? Remember how mercy blesses both the giver and the receiver? What about that?

You could even argue that her behaviour is more like Shylock's – once she has the upper hand she will push it as far as it will go.

The loss of Shylock's possessions is a savage blow on his life. What is worse, I would imagine, to a modern audience is the fact that Antonio insists that Shylock become a Christian! Many modern audience members would see that as going too far, that a man's faith and beliefs are his own business and that, to separate

Shylock from his faith and his people is a punishment that could never really be warranted. As a Christian, Shylock will not be allowed to live and mix with Jews. He will not be able to go into the Jewish area of Venice.

The tension in this scene is largely based on the image in the audience's minds of the knife cutting into Antonio's flesh, and for just a few moments, the audience is stealing itself (or already turning away) for the moment when the knife makes the incision. In most productions, Shylock has the knife poised above Antonio's chest and half the audience are watching through their fingers and on the verge of screaming by the time that Portia finally says 'Tarry' (wait).

But what follows is, for me, too much like bear-baiting, or some other 'sport' where the 'dog', the 'alien', the one who is different is tortured beyond self-respect and common decency.

An Elizabethan audience may well have found it more amusing. They might have believed that Shylock deserves it, that he has brought it on himself by refusing to show mercy to Antonio. They might have seen his conversion to Christianity as a positive development for him – now he would be able to attain eternal life in the Christian God. Antonio is doing him a favour.

I can't help, though, point out that this is the Elizabethan audience whose king (Henry VIII, Queen Elizabeth I's father) barely a generation before had gone completely against the then Christian Catholic Church and formed a new church (the Anglican Church) in order that he could divorce his legal wife and marry another woman (who turned out to be Elizabeth's mother, whom he later had executed). And, he went on to have *six* wives.

Imagine what might have happened to English history if the same rigid 'letter of the law' had been applied to him as is applied to Shylock in *The Merchant of Venice*.

This is the most important scene in the play. The effect it has on the audience will depend on the whole range of decisions that you make in constructing your production of the play (even if this production never has any existence anywhere outside of your own head.) The key questions are how to play Shylock and how to play Portia.

Are you satisfied enough with a Shylock who, for whatever reasons, is a misanthrope with no personal relations and is no better than an animal, prepared to cut the flesh off a living man for spite and revenge?

Are you satisfied with a Portia who comes into a court without any training and masquerading as a man? (Venice seems to have a lot of laws that apply to Shylock, is there a law against practising law without qualifications?) Who acts out a relentless vendetta on Shylock that can only be based on the belief that he is evil or less than human. As well, she deceives her husband in the masquerade and manipulates him into giving her the ring so that she can then question his love and have him believe that she has been unfaithful to him. Is this our heroine?

You need to think carefully about how you balance Shylock with the Venetians, in particular Portia, in order that your audience stays with you, engaged in the story and happy at the end.

ACT 4 SCENE 2 – VENICE

Portia and Nerissa go to Shylock's house to deliver the agreement which he must sign. Gratiano catches them and gives Portia the ring from Bassanio.

In an aside, Nerissa, still disguised, expresses the intention to extract a ring from her husband Gratiano. Portia predicts making much of the rings when they see their husbands.

Act 4 Scene 2 – Commentary

This scene is a continuation of scene 1, with perhaps a slight change of setting as this scene seems to be in the street.

Portia receives the ring from Bassanio and Jessica says she will get her ring from Gratiano, thus setting up the final scene of the play, in Act 5.

ACT 5 SCENE 1 – BELMONT

The scene begins with a dreamy and playful exchange between Lorenzo and Jessica, who again appear to be in perfect harmony with each other.

A messenger named Stephano enters, telling them that Portia will be arriving back before daybreak. Lorenzo says they must go in and prepare a welcome for her.

Lancelot arrives and, after pretending to not be able to see Lorenzo, says that Bassanio will be back by morning. Lorenzo, then, decides not to go in, but rather asks Stephano and the other musicians to play for them, which they do.

Portia and Nerissa arrive, followed soon by Bassanio and Gratiano. Gratiano is challenged by Nerissa about the whereabouts of the ring she had given him, and he tells her the truth that he has given it to the judge's clerk. Portia chastises Gratiano, telling him that she too gave Bassanio a ring. Gratiano defends himself by saying that Bassanio gave a ring to a judge that begged for it.

Portia is 'angered', saying that she won't come to Bassanio's bed until she sees the ring. Nerissa makes the same decision in regard to Gratiano. Bassanio tries to explain the context and just how much was owed to the doctor Balthasar for saving Antonio's life, but Portia accuses him of giving the ring to another woman. He says that in the circumstances, Portia would have begged him to give it to the doctor. (This is ironic, because, of course, she did beg him to give it to the doctor, herself!)

Portia responds that she will find this doctor and give herself to him – she won't deny him her body or her husband's bed. She continues: 'if I be left alone...I'll have that doctor for my bedfellow.' The audience realises that, because she *is* the doctor, what she is saying is that she will sleep by herself. But the meaning that Bassanio will take will be that she is going to sleep with Balthasar the young doctor of law.

Nerissa says she will do the same with the clerk, and Gratiano responds that he will 'mar the young clerk's pen'. (line 237) There is a pun here on 'pen' and 'penis', meaning that Gratiano will harm the young clerk's genitals if he sleeps with Nerissa.

Antonio intercedes on Bassanio's behalf, so Portia gives him 'another' ring to give to Bassanio. Bassanio recognises it as the ring she had given him before, that he had then given to the doctor.

The two women then taunt their husbands by saying that each slept with the man that their husband had given the ring to, and that's how they got the rings. Gratiano declares them cuckolded without deserving it. A 'cuckold' is a man whose wife has sex with other men.

At last, Portia tells them the truth – that she was the doctor and Nerissa the clerk. She offers the letter from Bellario as proof. Bassanio and Gratiano take the joke very well, Bassanio quipping that when he is away the doctor is welcome to sleep with his wife! (Seeing as they are the same person.)

Portia also has a letter for Antonio that tells him that all three of his ships have finally made it to shore safely. As well, she hands Lorenzo the guarantees from Shylock that ensure the inheritance of properties will go to him as Jessica's husband.

Portia suggests they go in and she and Nerissa will answer any questions the others have. Gratiano ends the play saying that he is keen to be 'couching with the doctor's clerk' (line 305) and declares that he will keep safe 'Nerissa's ring', punning on 'ring' as a reference to female genitals.

Act 5 Scene 1 Commentary

The play ends with a scene that is virtually entirely romantic comedy, and quite bawdy. Shylock and the issue of his treatment is completely forgotten, the only mention of him being that his money will be inherited by Lorenzo, his daughter's husband.

All three young couples are taken care of and the play ends with them in happiness.

Shakespeare opens the scene in an idyllic and dream-like tone, in total contrast to the bulk of Act 4. He wants to completely change the tone and concentrate on the love and the humour in this scene. He uses a poetic rhythm in the speeches of Lorenzo and Jessica that open the scene: 'The moon shines bright. In such a night as this, / When the sweet wind did gently kiss the trees'. (lines 1-2) The references to love stories of antiquity (Troilus, Cressida, Thisbe, Dido, Medea) place Lorenzo and Jessica into the realms of 'greatness' as lovers, as they tease each other about their honesty and commitment. The tone is serene but playful. This scene links nicely with the idea of storytelling to reflect different times and cultures.

The arrival of Portia, Nerissa, Bassanio and Gratiano brings the manufactured conflict over the rings. As in every other situation in the play, Portia has the upper hand, in this case because she knows something that her husband does not, that she was Balthasar, the young doctor.

The audience knows this too, so we have a situation of dramatic irony, that is sustained for quite some time. The longer it goes on for, the more daring the women become, taunting their husbands with the story that they got the rings back by sleeping with the two men in question. Of course, as the audience knows, this is true because they are in fact only saying that they slept with themselves, but the husbands must interpret their words as being an admission of infidelity.

It isn't the same in tone as what Portia did to Shylock in court, but it isn't entirely different either. The subject matter of the taunting becomes increasingly sexual, but eventually Portia lets the men off the hook by admitting that she was Balthasar and Nerissa the clerk. The play ends on a crude pun, characteristic of Gratiano.

The sheer cheekiness of what Portia and Nerissa do and the open sexuality of what they have their husbands believe would have been seen by the Elizabethan audience in the context of them being Venetian. Venetian women might behave in this manner, even if British wives would not. In that context, it is titillating and entertaining. Never forget, also, that in the Elizabethan theatre, female roles were played by young male actors. So, it is easy for Portia and Nerissa to look like young men.

A modern audience is usually expected to view it all in the context of feminism. They are women taking control and entering into a world of the law where they do not normally have access. On the facing page is a 19th century interpretation of Portia in full regalia of the period.

CONTEXT

William Shakespeare wrote *The Merchant of Venice* sometime between 1596 and 1598. As you have read above, this is during the historical period called Elizabethan England, after the monarch of the time, Queen Elizabeth I. This section in this study guide tells you about what kind of society Elizabethan England was, and some if the values, beliefs and practices of the period.

The Merchant of Venice is a play where we can say that the response of Shakespeare's own Elizabethan audience would have been different in certain aspects from an audience today. Following are some elements of the play, interpretations and presentations of which have changed over time due to context. This analysis of context will assist you in examining the different ways of interpreting the human experiences in the play over time.

Attitudes to and Treatment of Jews

Shylock is the play's main character and villain. Your edition of the play describes Elizabethan society as 'xenophobic'. This means that society was distrustful of people who were different. Racism is a form of xenophobia, but not the only one.

The prejudice against Jews, hatred in some cases, stems from the fact that it was the Jews who crucified Jesus Christ and who continue to deny the Christian belief that Jesus was/is the son of God. This has resulted in Christian societies conducting a vendetta against Jews. To an Elizabethan audience it was understood that the Jews were mistaken in their beliefs and that their only chance of eternal salvation was to be converted to Christians. For this reason, the ending which has Antonio insist that Shylock convert to Christianity is doing Shylock an enormous favour. This is because of the values and context of Elizabethan society.

Consequently, an Elizabethan audience would have accepted Shylock played as an absolute villain, doing evil for evil's sake. They also would have accepted a ghoulish 'cartoon' Shylock, the grossly ugly and twisted Jew who would enjoy nothing better than to cut out the flesh of a living man.

Attitudes have changed over time. This is especially true of this issue because of the persecution and attempted genocide of the Jews by the Nazis during World War II. These events, naturally, drew a lot of sympathy towards the Jews. This has tended to have a profound effect on the way *The Merchant of Venice* is performed these days. A recent (2004) film version begins with images of persecution of the Jews and injustices, so that the audience has these things in their minds before the play starts.

Modern productions have sought ways to humanise Shylock and make him more sympathetic. He has become a victim of xenophobia and an outcast from Venetian society. Sometimes, productions of the play have ended when Shylock leaves the stage at the end of Act 4 Scene 1, thus putting the emphasis on his defeat.

Modern audiences have a vastly different attitude to the instruction that Shylock becomes a Christian, seeing it as a theft of his soul and something that no one has the right to do to him. Due to shifts in values and context, this aspect of Shylock's treatment has gone from being regarded as a favour to being regarded as an atrocity.

Attitudes to Usury

Shylock is a usurer – a man who lends money for interest. Strange as it may seem to us, this was frowned upon in Elizabethan times. A gentleman might lend money to a friend, but he wouldn't charge interest.

Usury was associated with Jews. In Elizabethan England it was often difficult for Jews to finds other work.

To a modern audience, lending for interest is perfectly normal – try telling your local bank that it is ungentlemanly!

To an Elizabethan audience, you can see that the stereotypes associated with Jews and with usurers become interlinked to produce assumptions about the kind of man Shylock might be. They would expect him to be hated with no friends in Christian Venetian society. They would expect him to be obsessed with money and possessions.

A modern audience would have fewer assumptions, although the stereotype of Jews being 'tight' with money is still about and part of the stories that have incorrectly evolved over time about that culture.

Bonds and Contracts

Elizabethan audiences believed that Venetian law was very tight, tighter than English courts. It would have been within their expectation that a Venetian court would enforce a bond, even one that demanded the cutting of a pound of flesh. Elizabethan audiences seemed to have loved a court scene – your edition of the play says that a third of all plays of the era contain a court scene.

A modern audience, while still horrified at the thought of someone cutting out another's flesh, would also have the attitude that a contract, freely entered into by two adults, should be binding. A modern audience would expect a contract to hold and would likely have less sympathy for Bassanio and Antonio for entering into one.

The Status and Role of Women in Society

Portia is an interesting character, both in an Elizabethan context and a modern one. Like a good obedient daughter, she cooperates with the terms of her father's will and the test of the caskets as a means of choosing her husband. This gives the impression of her being submissive. But she is not submissive in any other way in the play.

In Act 1 Scene 2, she displays wit, sarcasm and a strong sense of self-worth in her amusing and denigrating descriptions of the men who have, up until then, come in search of her hand in marriage. She adopts disguise and saves the day in court, completely fooling everyone, including her new husband Bassanio. Then she taunts him for 'giving away' the ring he said he would always wear.

She is a much more active and assertive character than her male counterparts in the play. If we look at the women in Shakespeare's other comedies (Rosalind in *As You Like It* and Beatrice in *Much Ado About Nothing*), they are witty and assertive as well, but they submit to their husbands in the end. At the end of *The Merchant of Venice*, Portia is still leading everyone along. She has only just revealed that she was Balthasar and Nerissa the clerk and offers to 'explain all' during the evening.

Nerissa joins in all of Portia's assertive practices, and Jessica is positively rebellious to her own father, Shylock.

It is likely, also, that an Elizabethan audience would have seen the behaviour of these women in the context of them being Venetian. British women might not behave in this way, but Venetians were brazen and sophisticated.

For all these reasons, the play has readily lent itself to interpretation in the era of feminism. The three women in the play are feisty, and mostly non-submissive. Their deception of their husbands and subsequent bawdy taunting that they had cuckolded them can be seen as all a part of the battle of the sexes with the women asserting their right to be active participants in this battle.

SETTING

Over half of *The Merchant of Venice* is set in Venice. The rest is set in Belmont.

At the time of the writing of *The Merchant of Venice*, Venice was renowned as a republic of great wealth (due to trade), art, law and social stability. It also had the reputation of giving foreigners full access to its courts.

Shakespeare's audience would have expected Venice to be an affluent and sophisticated place. They would not have been likely to accept the idea of a contract for a pound of someone's flesh in a British setting. But in a Venetian setting, their impression that, as Portia says, even the Duke must respect the law would have made the situation more credible. In an English court, the judge could have simply thrown out the suggestion that one man had the right to cut out another's flesh. But the Duke does not have this jurisdiction – if the bond says 'a pound of flesh' then this must be respected.

Belmont, where Portia lives, is another city, now in Italy. The play says that Venice and Belmont are about twenty hours apart by coach. The real Belmont is in the south of Italy.

The play appears to be set at the time of its being written, near the end of the 16th century.

CHARACTERISATION

Shylock

Shylock is one of Shakespeare's best-remembered characters. Traditionally he is seen as a villain without a conscience, but more contemporary productions have tried to have him as more sympathetic.

The case against Shylock is that he is, firstly, that he is a 'usurer'. In our terms, a usurer is simply someone who lends money and charges interest in return. (Just like a bank.) The idea of lending money for interest is entirely entrenched in our culture and is a normal part of most people's lives.

But, in Shakespeare's day, usury was still viewed as 'un-gentlemanly' and an abuse. Gentlemen might lend money to their friends, but they would not charge interest. Usury, as well, was not controlled, so that the amount of interest charged was not regulated in any way, as it usually is in our culture. Usurers were seen as vultures preying on men who had come upon bad times, for whatever reasons.

Shakespeare doesn't exactly write a play that is a direct criticism of usury, but he does indulge in some of the stereotypes of a usurer in his creation of Shylock. Usurers care only about money. Usurers are generally hated. Usurers are not gentlemen. Usurers have no ethics.

On top of being a usurer, Shylock is a Jew. Venice, like Elizabethan England, is a Christian state. Jews are infidels, they do not believe what Christians believe – mainly that the man Jesus Christ was, and is, a God. Remember that the Jews crucified Christ, so not only did they not recognise his deity, they killed him, and in a manner most brutal. So, we might expect that Shylock would be a man prepared to take a knife and cut out the flesh of a living man. We might even associate this action with the crucifixion. Antonio isn't Christ, but he is, by all reports, a good man. He is a man prepared to die for the debt of his friend. He is *Christ-like*, and Shylock hates him.

Antonio is the 'opposite' of the usurer – he is prepared to put his own body and life at peril in order that his friend may have the money that he needs to woo his beloved Portia. Shylock the Jewish usurer, on the other hand, will lend Bassanio the money, but on the agreement that if the money is forfeited, he will have a pound of Antonio's flesh. Antonio lends out of generosity and love, while Shylock lends out of the desire to exploit and out of hatred. 'I am very glad of it. I'll plague him, I'll torture him. I am glad of it.' (3.1.91) Shakespeare juxtaposes Antonio with Shylock, greatly to Shylock's detriment.

Then there is the matter of Shylock's daughter, Jessica. She betrays her father and her race by eloping with Lorenzo, a Venetian Christian. There is no suggestion that she loves him because he is a Christian, but rather that love is a value that transcends these other considerations. But neither her actions, nor her words, reflect well on Shylock. She says: 'Alack, what heinous sin is it in me / To be ashamed to be my father's child!' (2.3.15), and there is a suggestion in her words that becoming a Christian is a kind of 'social climbing' in Venice. Generally, while she describes her feelings against her father as 'a heinous sin', the play does not disapprove of her actions. In fact, she and Lorenzo are one of the three romantic couples that make up the basis of the play's meaning about love. She describes living with her father as 'Our house is hell'. (2.3.2)

Perhaps more telling than this, are the remarks that Shylock himself makes about Jessica once she has eloped. He really does sound as though he cares more about the money, jewels and ring then he does about the loss of his daughter. 'I shall never see my gold again. Four score ducats at a sitting!' (3.1.86) She and the jewels are his possessions.

In the court-room scene, Shylock can be a ghoulish figure, eyes wide with anticipation and knife glistening. In the Elizabethan theatre, he could leer directly at the audience, and play up to their horror at what he is about to do. In a modern theatre, costume and make-up can emphasise his 'alien' qualities in Venetian society. Lighting can be used to make him look cold and sinister if you like, or as a figure from a horror movie, or a pathological killer.

The view of Shylock as a man obsessed with possessions and wealth is challenged by his behaviour in the courtroom. Near the outset, Bassanio offers him double what he is owed, 'For thy three thousand ducats, here is six'. (4.1.85) Later Portia offers him three times the amount he is owed. Shylock does not give either of these offers the slightest consideration, responding that he would not

accept even six times six thousand ducats, 'I would have my bond.' (4.1.87)

This suggests to us very strongly that Shylock is really motivated more deeply by something other than money. He hates Antonio, but is that enough? Isn't it more likely, and more dramatically powerful, if his anger is directed at Venetian society in general? The society that calls him 'dog' and spits at him for being what he is and believing what he does. At 4.1.89 Shylock makes a speech in which he basically accuses Venetian society of hypocrisy. He points out that Venetians keep and use slaves which they have bought. 'Shall I say to you, / "Let them be free! Marry them to your heirs!"' (4.1.93) and so on. 'The pound of flesh which I demand of him / Is dearly bought; 'tis mine, and I will have it.' (4.1.99) He is arguing that, just as Venetians do as they please with their slaves, and would mock any suggestions he might make about how they treat their slaves, so he will do what he likes with what he has bought – the pound of Antonio's flesh.

In fact, Shylock challenges the Duke to make a mockery, if he chooses, of Venetian law – 'If you deny me, fie upon your law'. (4.1.101) In other words, the bond is a legal contract, so to deny it would be to question all contracts in Venice.

Portia's entry (as Balthasar, the young doctor of law) and her first remarks accord with Shylock's purpose – she says that there is no lawful way that Shylock can be denied the payment of his bond. He even praises her: 'O wise young judge, how I do honour thee!' She offers him three times the money, in the name of mercy, but he refuses.

And she has him 'dig himself in' deeper in brutality by refusing to allow a surgeon (doctor) to attend Antonio's imminent bleeding because it is not written into the contract. Then she leads him to the brink of murder, to the brink of most amoral brutality: 'A sentence: come, prepare' (4.1.300) he says with the knife poised just above Antonio's chest (and the audience held in anticipation).

It is here that Portia interrupts Shylock with 'Tarry a little' and proceeds to strip him of everything, including his dignity and his faith.

Shylock gets what he deserves? The audience delights in his diminishing and feels vindicated.

Shylock is treated too harshly? The audience feels sympathy for him.

Before I get to these questions, I want to pose another: Do we know what Shylock's *real* intentions are? If Portia had not interrupted him with 'Tarry a little...', would he, in fact have carved the knife into Antonio's chest? Or was it his real intention to push as far as he could towards embarrassing the Venetians and their law, then put down the knife and accept the three, or six, or nine thousand ducats?

What do you think and how can we tell?

The text itself leaves this question open because it does not take us quite to the point where Shylock must *act*. Sure, he has plenty to say and he has done a fine impersonation of a man who might kill another, but will he actually do it? Well, we will never know, because Portia speaks up.

So, we must look to the text for indications of whether he is the kind of man who would kill, or is he the kind of man who would play an elaborate practical joke on a culture he hates and who hates him. The answer to this is to be found, like everything about a play, in the playing.

In Act 4 Scene 1, the courtroom scene, we can easily have Shylock play the 'villain' in an exaggerated, almost comic, way. He can take the audience into his confidence with winks and nods and other facial expressions that will suggest to the audience that he will never really cut Antonio, but he will wield his power while he has it, for his own satisfaction and amusement. He will stand with his knife poised above Antonio's chest, about to let everyone off, but Portia interrupts him.

Or, we can play him as a man whose humanity has been diminished by a lifetime of racist slurs and bigotry. That this treatment has resulted in producing a man who can and will slice another man's chest open and carve flesh.

Or, we can play him as the complete villain. He can be able to cut Antonio because he is evil and there is nothing that he is not capable of doing. It may well be that this is how he was played in Shakespeare's day. A Jew, who does not believe in Christ or the true Christian God, might have, to an English Elizabethan audience, no moral qualms about slicing someone up.

Even the most villainous Shylock may draw *some* sympathy from the audience when he is stripped of all of his possessions, his dignity and even forced to deny his people and change his religion. Here we need to think about how his experiences and the prejudices of the period affect the way in which he engages with the world around him. Shylock must be motivated by experiences he faced and the assumptions people make about his culture.

It is an interesting and telling example of what we now tend to refer to as *context*, that the impact on audiences of the demand that Shylock become a Christian has changed utterly. An Elizabethan audience would have been able to view it as a kind of favour – Shylock is being forced to embrace the 'true' Christian religion and, thus, his soul will be saved. After Shylock's appalling behaviour, good Antonio has done him the service of insisting that he take on the faith of the true Christian God and the saviour Jesus Christ.

But a modern audience is likely to view the instruction that Shylock turn Jew as the most severe and unfair of all the consequences of his behaviour. To require that a man reject his culture and change his religion is in fact illegal in a lot of countries. Some would regard it as an impossible requirement, the kind of thing that one could comply with on the outside but never on the inside.

Shylock and 3.1.42-57

The answer to Shylock is likely to come from his great and most important speech at 3.1.42-57.

Salarino theorises that Shylock will not take the flesh because it is of no use - 'What's that good for?' (line 41)

Shylock's response is 'To bait a fish withal; if it will feed nothing else, it will feed my revenge.' (line 42) The remark about the fish is a 'throwaway', he might do anything with it. But his mind is really on *revenge*. If we take Antonio as representing Venetian society, then that is where Shylock's anger comes from.

'I am a Jew. Hath not a Jew eyes?' (line 46) Here Shylock begins his appeal for tolerance based on a series of rhetorical questions, that point to the fact that Jews are human in the same ways as Christians. If the audience answers (in silence) 'yes' to these questions, then perhaps a message of common humanity may be communicated.

But Shylock plays a trick on his audience (on the stage and off) by turning his last question away from the utopian images of common humanity to the very human practice of revenge. 'And if you wrong us, shall we not revenge?' (line 52) He says that if a Jew wrongs a Christian, then the Christian will seek revenge, therefore if a Jew is wronged by a Christian, then the Jew will seek revenge. And he intends to do so: 'The villainy you teach me I will execute, and it shall go hard but I will better the instruction.' (line 56) In other words, I will be even more villainous than you Christians who have taught me to be a villain. This is very much a threat. And it's a big threat, because Jews had, since the time of Christ been hated and treated as second-class citizens for having crucified Christ.

How are you going to have your Shylock perform this speech? Is he angry all the way through? Is he desperate to be understood? When he says 'Hath not a Jew eyes?', will the audience feel compassion for him? At the end, is he bitter or just determined? Or is his tone of voice even and calm throughout, as though he is just stating things as they are, without emotion?

This speech can be the centre of the play. It comes at about the halfway point, anyway. It can be the speech that the audience remember as being the key to understanding Shylock. If your Shylock is a murderer, then this speech tells us why. He is taking revenge for all Jews who have been the subjects of bigotry. If your Shylock is a trickster not a murderer, then this speech shows his trickery, his delight in fooling the Christians. If your Shylock is sympathetic, then he will have won the audience's sympathy in this speech. They might even find him justified in his intentions.

How would I have Shylock in my production?

I would have him world weary and cynical. He accepts the loan bond with Antonio and Bassanio because he likes to have young Christians under his control; he likes the feeling of power.

Jessica's betrayal and defection to Christianity hurts him very badly and makes him angry. He vents this anger on Antonio when he hears that he might default.

My Shylock will not really cut Antonio's flesh, but enjoys the lead up to the decision and enjoys the near-victory in court. His 'punishment' is too great, especially him being forced to become Christian. At the end he is a pathetic figure, a symbol of the triumph of prejudice. The audience feels his suffering and looks with a jaundiced eye on the foolery of the young Venetian lovers, especially Portia who showed no mercy either and Gratiano whose baiting of Shylock with insulting remarks show him to be a racist bore.

Portia

When we first meet Portia she is in the grips of a lottery for her to find a husband according to conditions set out in her father's will. These conditions have it that suitors must choose one of three caskets, one gold, one silver and one lead. If they choose the one that contains a small portrait of Portia, then they get her hand in marriage. If they choose incorrectly, they must leave immediately and promise never to marry at all. This is the stuff of fairy tales.

Just the same, Act 1 Scene 2, where she and Nerissa discuss the rather motley collection of suitors that have come to her so far, is a delightful and amusing scene. Our initial impression of Portia is that she is witty and articulate. We could find her somewhat conceited, if she is played in that way.

Many critics have pointed out that as independent and intelligent a young woman as Portia would be unlikely to co-operate with the device of the caskets to find a husband, but she does so out of loyalty to her father. We are meant to accept that, in his wisdom, he has reasoned that superficial men will choose the gold or silver and only a wise man will choose the lead, where the portrait is. Luckily, this lottery throws up Bassanio, who she genuinely wants as her husband, and he does in fact choose the right leaden casket.

Portia is playful and witty throughout these parts of the play as a Prince from Morocco, and then one from Arragon, try and fail to choose correctly. Most productions play Morocco and Arragon as arrogant overblown fools, so that Portia's disingenuous and sarcastic manner don't so much come across as conceit. Even an Elizabethan audience would have felt that she deserved the right to choose her own husband and would have been pleased that she gets who she wants anyway (Bassanio). Perhaps her father knew something after all. The audience admires her adherence to her father's slightly 'off-beat' approach to matrimonial matchmaking.

Like many of Shakespeare's romantic heroines, she is quick to don men's clothing when the opportunity presents itself, and boasts about how well she will be able to masquerade as a man, even when dealing with her husband Bassanio.

It doesn't really surprise us that she is a good lawyer; she has already showed herself to be articulate and quick-thinking. Even so, the sheer eloquence and melody of her famous speech on mercy, comes as a delightful surprise. (4.1.180) In the imagery, mercy is 'the gentle rain from heaven'. Perhaps the most persuasive part is the claim that it is 'twice blest' because it blesses the one that gives mercy and the one that receives it.

Many critics have pointed out, that, having delivered a beautiful speech on the efficacy of mercy, Portia proceeds to show no mercy at all towards Shylock. She tricks him into trusting her (Balthasar) and then takes from him everything he has, including his pride and his culture. So much for mercy.

She then (still as Balthasar) harangues Bassanio until he gives her the ring, that she had given him and had him promise never to take off. This sets up the humour of the last Act, where Portia and Nerissa berate their respective husbands for the rings that they have given away - to Balthasar and his clerk, who are Portia and Nerissa anyway.

She is quite bawdy in her threats to sleep with whoever has the ring and claims that she has already done so. Eventually she tells Bassanio the truth.

Portia is supposed to be a witty and delightful character. She may be a pre-feminist in the sense that she maintains control over her relationships with men and she proves that a woman can do a man's job in court. When things are looking bad for Bassanio's friend Antonio, she dresses up as a man and becomes an amateur lawyer – she takes control like some kind of super-woman.

The problem is that she also has some fairly 'dirty work' to do on Shylock, which she does with a gusto that might offend some. Bassanio and even Antonio prove to be more inclined to mercy than Portia does.

Antonio

The play begins with a speech by Antonio about his melancholia. 'In sooth I know not why I am so sad.' (1.1.1) Solanio and Salarino suggests that he is worried about business and his ships at sea, which he denies, then they say he must be in love, which he scoffs at.

Most of the commentary about Antonio has to do with this – is he the model of a good friend to Bassanio, or is he in fact in love with him?

Antonio is everyone's (except Shylock's) idea of a fine and honourable Venetian man. He is prepared to go into debt, enter a bond for a pound of his flesh, and ultimately die without complaint, for his friend Bassanio.

If he is the model of nobility and friendship, how does this sit with the fact that he is hated by Shylock for having spat on him, called him names and all the rest, because Shylock is a Jew. In other words, if Shylock is to be believed, Antonio is a racist.

As for his being in love with Bassanio, the fact that he uses the word 'love' in connection with his feelings about Bassanio does not tell us much as the word was used more liberally between men in Elizabethan times. The passage that is most interesting is Act 4 Scene 1 when Bassanio says that it should be him who pays the bond to Shylock, not Antonio. Antonio says: 'I am a tainted wether of the flock, / Meetest for death; the weakest kind of fruit / Drops earliest to the ground, and so let me.' (4.1.115) He is saying that he is the weakest, so he should die. What does he mean by this? The 'wether' is a castrated ram. He could be referring to the fact that he has no children, or perhaps that he will never have children, because he will not engage in a heterosexual relationship. His reference to weakness in the image of the 'weakest kind of fruit' could be a reference to homosexuality I suppose, or just to his melancholia.

Whether or not, he is certainly a noble and self-sacrificing friend, whose values are based on honour.

Bassanio

Bassanio is liked by both Portia and Antonio, so something about him inspires affection in others.

Our first impression of him is that he is irresponsible and has spent money that didn't belong to him so that his friend Antonio is forced to enter into a foolish outrageous bond in order that Bassanio can seek the hand of Portia.

The best thing he does is that he chooses the right casket and therefore wins Portia, as she had wished. In choosing the lead casket, he has demonstrated that he is not fooled by appearances. He is therefore the kind of man her father would have wanted for her, thus demonstrating the efficacy of the test of the caskets as set out by the father.

He does try to offer Shylock extra money in lieu of the flesh, and he does offer to be cut instead of Antonio, but over all our impression of him is that he is lucky to have the people around him that he does. Also, he is prepared to accept Shylock's deals once he knows he cannot shed any blood, but Portia stops him. This suggests to us that he is a more tolerant and forgiving person than she is.

The play loves lovers and he is one of them. He seems agreeable, without having a well-defined character.

Gratiano

His friends seem to regard him as a jokester who talks too much. The audience has to decide how to react to his insults directed at Shylock, because they are very much a feature of his speech. 'O be thou damned, inexecrable dog', 'thy currish spirit', 'wolfish, bloody, starved, and ravenous', are all from 4.1. He seems especially angered at Shylock, saying that if he had been judge, Shylock would have been hung not turned into a Christian.

He is also the purveyor of ribaldry. 'Thanks i'faith, for silence is only commendable / in a neat's tongue dried, and a maid not vendible.' (1.1.111) These are references to a sexually impotent male and a sexually unattractive woman. He ends the whole play on a crude pun about his wife Nerissa's genitals. We can imagine that this line would be accompanied by some leering and winking perhaps, or some other course stage business.

His language toward Shylock and his ribald jokes are both rather out of step with today's values, so there may be a problem presenting him in a modern production. He is supposed to be a good friend and an amusing man. If you want, in your production to present the Venetians as morally flawed, Gratiano will be a part of that.

Lorenzo

Lorenzo is the friend of Gratiano but he is much quieter. He and Jessica (Shylock's daughter) elope and exist in harmony on the occasions that we see them.

He does not seem bothered by the fact that she is Jewish, and neither does anyone else. What this suggests is that those characters who we accuse of being anti-Jew may be merely anti-Shylock.

Jessica

Jessica, Shylock's daughter, is beautiful by all accounts and when we meet her she craves to escape from the cloying misery of the environment of her father's house.

She does so by eloping with Lorenzo, taking quite a bit of money and some jewellery with her. She does seem aware of the seriousness of what she feels about her father, as she says, in the play's only soliloquy: 'Alack, what heinous sin it is in me / To be ashamed to be my father's child!'

She is such a likeable character that such a remark reflects more on Shylock than it does on herself. She craves to be a Christian and Lorenzo's wife. Once she is, she seems protected from the play's suffering and serious side. She does not sit through the ordeal of the court scene, but rather is with Lorenzo, happily minding Portia's house while she is gone. Her father's ruin has no effect on her.

Like the other young women of the play, she is independent-minded and takes control of her own life in leaving her father.

Nerissa

As 'waiting gentlewoman' to Portia, she follows her mistress in all things. She supports her rather as a friend would, during the process of the choosing of a husband by the mechanism of the caskets.

In Act 4 she dresses as a clerk for the court scene and fools her recently wed husband Gratiano into giving her (him) a ring that Gratiano had promised never to part with. All of this, of course, is by way of mimicking what Portia is doing.

Her title as 'gentlewoman' is presumably what makes her a satisfactory match for Gratiano, who is a gentleman of Venice.

The audience will be won over to her in the delightful and amusing Act 1 Scene 2, where she and Portia discuss the motley and unattractive group of suitors that have come thus far for Portia's hand.

While some might find Gratiano rather brutish, he and Nerissa are two of the six lovers in the play and the play delights in their love. His final line, which is a punning reference to her ring and her genitals, is supposed to amuse, but on stage we can have her respond in any way that we see consistent with her character. She can be scandalised, disapproving or non-comprehending, for example.

Like Portia and Jessica, she is likely to be played as a 'feisty' and independent-minded woman.

Salanio and Salarino

In Act 1 Scene 1, they are hanging around with Antonio, offering explanations for him as to why he is so melancholy. It would be easy to play them as 'fops', the Elizabethan term for men who are less 'manly', more effeminate than others and care more about clothes and a fastidious appearance. Fops, in Shakespeare, are by no means always homosexual (for example, Roderigo in *Othello*) but a modern audience might interpret them in that way.

IDEAS

This section will deal with the ideas in the play and the values that the play highlights. Of course we will deal with human experiences specifically but also take an in-depth examination of several ideas as these illustrate different aspects of the human experience and the concepts within it.

Human Experiences

In *The Merchant of Venice* we see much about the human experience and these aspects such as xenophobia, love, friendship and revenge are covered in detail below. In terms of the rubric we see a variety of human experiences in this text and many are extremely emotional such as the court scene and when Shylock's daughter runs away with a Christian. The Venetian attitude to Shylock is consistent with the assumptions and attitudes of the time and we don't see this change throughout the play. While the Venetians as a group are unable to change or adapt their ideas generally they are more tolerant for love and Jessica seems to be exempted from the general wariness and spite around the Jews.

It is of interest to us here that the stories that have built up in society about the Jewish faith and their money-lending has an impact on the narrative and Shakespeare makes use of this. These stories reinforce the stereotypes of the Jews and Shakespeare plays on this knowledge that he assumes of his audience. Is the conclusion and making Shylock convert to Christianity a way of helping him see the world differently or is it the xenophobic tradition reinforced, or both? The ideas around the Jewish faith are consistent in the play and yet modern audiences may see them as paradoxical in that these attitudes aren't very Christian. Now let's have a look at these ideas in detail.

Xenophobia

Traditionally, Shylock is the villain of the play. He is the hated figure who is prepared to call on an outrageous bond and actually cut a pound of flesh from a living man's body. The audience will fear and hate him and be relieved when his desire to cut into Antonio's chest is thwarted by Portia.

But the question is: Does Shylock become the villain of the play because of personal traits, or is he a villain by dint of his race? Are these qualities that the audience is supposed to dislike, stereotypical Jewish characteristics? Is he evil because he is Jewish? How does the text represent human qualities and emotions associated with, or arising from, these experiences that Shylock has endured?

When we discuss how the play was performed and received in Shakespeare's day, we are of course guessing. But our best guess is that Elizabethan audiences resented and distrusted Jews. Their stereotypical Jew would have been just like Shylock – ugly, unpopular, obsessed with money, a father too strict, and lacking in basic human dignity, because of the flawed nature of his religion. To an Elizabethan audience, Jews made the fatal mistake of not believing in the divinity of Christ and of having crucified him some 1600 years before. This made Jews guilty of an atrocity and damned to miss out on Christian salvation. Jews had no moral code because they did not have Christian principles upon which to base it. Therefore, a Jew would cut the flesh out of a man, causing death.

Shylock is exactly what the Elizabethans would have expected in a Jew. The conclusion we can draw here is that the play itself is anti-Semitic, or xenophobic. At the very least, it reinforces xenophobia.

But, can the play be not xenophobic? Can we perform this play in such a way that Shylock is no longer a stereotypical Jew, a walking reinforcement of Elizabethan xenophobia?

Well, yes.

Many productions, especially in the last hundred years, have tried to be so. To reduce this process to its elements, it will involve shifting the balance of sympathy from the Venetians to Shylock, to at least some extent. We don't have to make Shylock loveable, that would be ridiculous. But we might make him sympathetic, a victim, a product of generations of prejudice and abuse. At the very least we need to make Shylock a product of his environment, rather than someone who is simply inherently evil. This isn't difficult to do when we consider that Shylock reports that he is spat on, called a dog and so on in the street.

Can we make Shylock sympathetic? Yes, much of what happens to him in the play is pitiable. His daughter leaves him to elope with a Christian and she even steals money and jewellery from him. He is a solitary figure with no real friends. Tubal is polite towards him, not affectionate, and he just might be enjoying raising Shylock's anxiety over the money that Jessica is spending.

Shylock goes into the courtroom scene with what he believes is the upper hand. He taunts the Venetians with the demand that he will have his pound of Antonio's flesh. I have argued above that it would be possible to play Shylock as not really intending to take Antonio's flesh, but that Portia stops him before he can stop himself.

But, in any case, this scene turns out to be one of gradual destruction of Shylock – he even loses his dignity, having to beg the Duke for his life, and his culture, being forced to turn Christian. For a modern audience, his fall is dramatic and perhaps more than he deserves – having your culture taken away from you might be more than anyone deserves. So, we can readily make the audience feel at least pity for Shylock.

The other side of the equation is to throw a more critical eye over the Christian Venetians in the play. This, in my opinion, is very easy to do. Except for Antonio, they are an idle bunch, with an easy affluence that doesn't require work. They can readily be presented as hedonistic, seeking pleasure wherever – in the carnival and in love. Bassanio, by his own admission has been irresponsible with money.

Shylock tells us that Antonio has abused him because he is Jewish. Gratiano does so as well. Portia finds foreign suitors unattractive and inadequate. As Christians, there is not a single Christian principle in sight, except for Antonio's willingness to die for his friend and beloved. And, most of all, when Portia has Shylock under her control in the courtroom, she ramps up the punishment and cultural abuse, rather than showing any of her own apparently beloved mercy.

If we get the audience to sympathise with (or even just understand) Shylock, then it follows that they will question the need to treat him with such cruelty and vengeance.

Instead of being, itself, xenophobic, the play becomes a study of xenophobia and its effect on a society. It is most powerfully an examination of the effects of being on the receiving end of xenophobia. Shylock is the product of moral outrage, revenge and intolerance, all based on xenophobia. If he is a man capable of slicing the flesh of another, then it is because of his treatment by the Venetian Christians. This interpretation of *The Merchant of Venice*, makes it a bigger play.

Shylock's speech at 3.1.42-57 becomes truly the centre of the play, as Shylock promises to wreak a fearful vengeance on Venetian Christian society, using Antonio as a scapegoat: 'The villainy you teach me I will execute, and it shall go hard but I will better the instruction.' Jews have eyes and hearts and so on, just like Christians, and they will take revenge also – just like Christians, or worse.

Love

All of Shakespeare's comedies are about love. *The Merchant of Venice* is by no means a typical comedy, and its treatment of the theme of love isn't typical either. Love is a crucial element of human experience and Shakespeare allows us to see several perspectives on it in the play.

For one thing, most of the comedies end in marriage, whereas in this play the marriages occur well before the end of the play. This is quite a significant structural shift, as the usual structure is one of love developing in spite of difficulties and challenges, culminating in marriage at the end as the triumph of love. Here, Lorenzo and Jessica marry very soon after we learn about their love, and the other two couples are wed by the end of Act 3, before the most important action of the play.

Love itself is the focus, with less attention being on marriage as the proof and culmination of love. In fact, early in the play, marriage is a kind of game of chance (the caskets), with little to do with love. The shrewdness of Portia's father's device is that it chooses the wise man who is not fooled by appearances. The magic is that it chooses the very man that she has already fallen in love with (Bassanio).

All three of our couples fall in love quickly, but seem to fall wisely. It is as though love is out there, complete and perfect, all you have to do is find the right person. In *The Merchant of Venice* also, love is not bothered by what we might call 'distractions'. Bassanio and Gratiano are shocked to hear that their wives were with them in court as Balthasar and his clerk, but they don't seem bothered about it. They respond as very good sports when it is revealed that these fellows that have 'slept' with their wives (Balthasar and the clerk, again) are in fact their wives themselves. Gratiano gets in a bawdy pun about his wife's genitals and everyone seems fine about the whole thing.

What we see in all of this is that love is able to withstand all sorts of distractions and challenges. This is not always true of the human experience.

In a sense, Jessica and Lorenzo withstand the greatest challenge in that they must elope and Jessica must betray her father, but things go remarkably smoothly for them. The opening passage of the last scene of the play, shows them in idyllic circumstances, the happiest of lovers. They are not touched at all by Shylock's destruction; in fact they happily accept the financial benefits of it to them.

The play doesn't tell us much about the nature of love – it comes quickly and it is resilient. Rather it celebrates love and raises up those who love.

Friendship (and Antonio's Love)

Antonio is the model of friendship. For his friend Bassanio, he is prepared to enter into a bond for a pound of his own flesh, effectively his life. When it looks as though he is going to have to pay the forfeit, he is noble and calm. His friendship is firm.

If Antonio's friendship is in fact love for Bassanio, then Antonio's love is surely the strongest in the play. 'I think he only loves the world for him' (2.8.51) says Solanio about Antonio's love for Bassanio. His calm demeanour in the courtroom scene is largely to reassure Bassanio that he will submit to Shylock's knife without fear. His speech 'I am a tainted wether of the flock' can be read as an admission of his unusual sexuality, the passion of his love for Bassanio. Antonio's love, unlike Gratiano's for example is selfless and unpossessive love.

Antonio loves Bassanio, but he gives him up to Portia.

Appearance and Reality

This is what the device of the caskets is all about. Both Morocco and Arragon mistakenly equate outward beauty with inward value. Only Bassanio recognises the fact that outer beauty does not necessarily reflect inward beauty.

'The world is still deceived with ornament', he says. (3.2.74) And: 'Thus ornament is but the guiled shore / To a most dangerous sea.' So, he argues that what is attractive on the outside wides ugliness or danger inside.

This is all very well, for the matter of choosing caskets, but what about his love herself. Portia is reputed the most beautiful, and she is rich as well! Shouldn't the lesson he is teaching about appearances here, reflect on the inner beauty of his most outwardly beautiful Portia?

Well, it doesn't seem to. And what about Shylock? Wouldn't you say that he is a 'lead casket' if ever there was one. Everyone judges him on his appearance, and they seem to be reinforced for doing so.

If the message of the caskets is this contrast between appearance and reality, then surely we should be most suspicious of the three women in the play, all reportedly beautiful. And, indeed, each of them proves quite capable of dishonesty. Portia and Nerissa distort the relationship between appearance and reality by disguising themselves as men and going to court. Effectively, they become men because their contribution to the trial is as a man's would have been. Portia is confident enough to contradict Bassanio.

Jessica deceives her father in eloping and she too uses disguise (as a page) as a means of this deception.

Each of these women ends the play in a state of delirious happiness, so there appears to be no consequence to their deception.

Mercy

Portia's famous set piece on mercy in Act 4 Scene 1 is a lyrical homily on a quality that is a particularly Christian principle, and one of the stated attributes of the Christian God. 'It is an attribute to God himself'. (line 190)

For all this, there is precious little mercy on display in the play. Portia's speech, in fact, draws attention to the fact that there is no mercy shown. It is like a poetic advertisement for mercy, but no one much is getting any. This is a pity, as it is, of course, 'twice blest'!

Arguably, the Duke shows mercy towards Shylock when he allows him to live when he could have had him executed for being an alien threatening the life of a citizen of Venice.

Portia does give Shylock one chance to choose mercy for Antonio, and thus, one assumes, earn some for himself. 'We do pray for mercy, / And that same prayer doth teach us all to render / The deeds of mercy' (line 196) says Portia, but Shylock does not listen – 'I crave the law'.

So Shylock shows no mercy to Antonio. And Portia, though she has eloquently made the case for mercy, will show none to Shylock in return. This is most unlike the Christian principles she espoused only moments before. In fact, her actions are more like revenge, that most unchristian of practices. Think about what these moments show us about human experiences and the effect of social mores on the way people behave.

Revenge

Shylock sees the Christian treatment of Jews as revenge — revenge for the murder of their God, Jesus Christ. His central speech at 3.1.42-57 appears to argue for the common humanity of all, on the grounds that we all have eyes, a nose, a heart and so on. But when Shylock gets to revenge, it becomes clear that he is not arguing for mutual understanding, but for an escalation of hostilities. He will take revenge in a way that will take account of what Christians have taught him about revenge.

In the last part of 4.1, the courtroom scene, revenge is enacted upon Shylock by Portia especially, with the support of Gratiano, though less so from Bassanio, her unwitting husband.

Portia turns out to be a more powerful revenger than Shylock, as she strips him of his dignity and his culture. Of interest to us here is the fact that revenge is a strong motivator and an emotion that heavily weighs on individual's decision-making processes.

Justice and the Judiciary

Elizabethan audiences are said to have loved a court scene and to also have been interested in law and the way that courts were conducted.

English law allowed for two kinds of justice. There were common law courts where matters were settled by judgements based on statutes or precedent - that is, according to the letter of the law, or according to how things had been decided in the past. This is the kind of system that is operating in Venice, in the play. In England, there was also Chancery Court, where the Lord Chancellor ruled on the basis of equity and conscience, in other words 'natural justice'. A court of this latter kind could have ruled that Shylock accept the money and Antonio keep his body intact, because that outcome would be seen as 'justice'. A court like the former one could only uphold the law and refer to precedent. As there was no precedent, or all it said was that contracts must be honoured, this could not help Antonio. The only one who could let Antonio off the hook was Shylock.

So, the relationship between justice and law is not as clear as you might have hoped. A just outcome to the matter, from our point of view, would surely have been for Shylock to get his money, plus maybe a bit more for it being late, and Antonio to keep his chest. But this was something that the Duke could not determine, as Portia says. The court system may not be in everyone's experience but in this case it is a crucial scene and the representation of it makes the play. While the letter of the law is upheld do we get justice? Are the lives and culture reinforced or are assumptions challenged? It seems that the prejudices and status quo are preserved and the eventual loser is Shylock but you may differ in your analysis.

The Tragic Drift

In all of Shakespeare's comedies, there is a point at which things are in a precarious state, and there is the potential for things to end in tragedy. In this, Shakespeare is suggesting that happiness and sadness in life are never very far away. What turns out well, may not necessarily have done so. In the comedies, there is a natural resolution of conflict — conflict which might well have not been resolved. It is as though comedy and tragedy have very similar elements, but one exists in a universe that is benign and the other in a universe that is malevolent, where happiness is impossible.

The Merchant of Venice has a strong drift towards tragedy. At the moment when Shylock's knife is poised above Antonio's chest, the tragedy is very close, until Portia stops it with the word 'Tarry'. The potential for tragedy never comes that close in any other play.

As well there is disagreement and complexity as to whether we might consider Shylock's fate as tragic anyway. It seems to me that this would require the cutting, or severe modification of Act 5. This would be obviously  against the original intentions behind the play. Shylock's fate may well hang over Act 5, but I believe that we are intended to celebrate love with the three couples, in spite of it.

DRAMATIC TECHNIQUES

Dramatic Irony

Dramatic Irony occurs when the audience knows more than one or more of the characters of the play.

Shakespeare uses dramatic irony in all his plays, but especially the comedies. For example, every time a character goes in disguise there is a lot of dramatic irony because the audience knows the character is in disguise and the other characters do not. This can create humour and it can give rise to the situation where the disguised reveals something about himself that the audience will understand but the other characters will not.

In *The Merchant of Venice*, most of Act 4 and most of Act 5 have dramatic irony operating. When Balthasar and his clerk enter the court, we know that they are Portia and Nerissa, but no one else does. One immediate element of this is that they are women taking roles in a courtroom that women would not normally be able to do, and doing them well. The audience will be aware of this. This effectively may challenge the stereotypes about women in the culture of the audience.

Another aspect is the humour and irony of their interaction with characters they know, and who normally know them, in this case their husbands. It is an absolute convention of the disguise in Shakespeare that disguised characters are never recognised. And so it is here. Portia and Nerissa interact with their husbands without being detected.

Portia even contradicts Bassanio on three occasions in the court. This might greatly amuse some audiences. It also can be seen as challenging stereotypes about male-female relationships, depending again on the culture of the audience.

As for Nerissa, like Portia she engages in conversation with her husband after the trial and manages to extract from him the ring that she had given him and he had promised never to remove.

Due to dramatic irony, the audience may be amused by this, and would know that it is a set up for more humour later in the play.

This 'later in the play' occurs in the next scene, Act 5 Scene 1, when Portia and Nerissa demand that their husbands explain the whereabouts of the rings, that the audience knows they in fact have. This whole routine, as Portia and Nerissa tease and taunt their husbands with the statement that they have each slept with the men that were given the rings, is based on dramatic irony. The audience understands that when they say they slept with these men, they are really saying that they slept with themselves, because they *are* the men who have the rings!

So, most of the humour in Act 5 is based on dramatic irony.

The Climax

The well-made play is said to have a climax about exactly where the one in *The Merchant of Venice* is – about three-quarters the way through the play. In fact, few of Shakespeare's plays have so distinct a climax as this play.

It comes, of course, in Act 4, in the famous courtroom scene. This is the scene we have been waiting for since Act 1 when Antonio agreed to enter into a bond the forfeit of which would be the taking of a pound of his flesh. The very entry into such an outrageous contract has the audience expecting to see it carried out.

Shakespeare builds the climax well during this scene. It begins with the duke telling Antonio that he feels sorry for him because Shylock his adversary is 'an inhuman wretch, / Uncapable of pity'. (4.1.3-4) Antonio states his intention to meet Shylock's rage with a calm and quiet spirit.

This has prepared us for Shylock's entry. When he does enter, he is addressed by the Duke who asks him to give a 'gentle answer, Jew'. But Shylock rages, saying that his only reason for proceeding is that he hates Antonio. He goes on to accuse the Venetians of hypocrisy as he will treat Antonio's flesh as they treat their servants which they have bought and own.

Bassanio begs to be substituted for Antonio, but Antonio disagrees, saying that he is the weaker and should die, not Bassanio.

Portia and Nerissa enter, Portia with a letter for the Duke from Bellario. From here, Portia, as Balthasar, takes control of proceedings. She makes her beautiful appeal for mercy, but Shylock is unmoved. He is becoming increasingly unreasonable and has the knife out and ready to be used.

Bassanio tries to convince the Duke to rule against Shylock's bond, but Portia howls him down, saying that an impossible precedent would be set that would plague Venetian law. Shakespeare builds the tension as there is further back and forth talk between Portia, Shylock and then Antonio's moving (and loving to Bassanio) 'last words'.

Throughout, Portia argues that the law can do nothing and the bond must be honoured. The tension becomes unbearable, as Antonio lies waiting, his chest bare, for the knife.

The absolute climax comes when Shylock is over Antonio, the knife poised, just above his skin, when...'Tarry a little' says Portia and breaks the tension. It is a moment of great theatre.

Structure

The pattern of building to the climax is an aspect of structure. The climax is powerful, and the resolution comes quickly after it, then Shylock is gone. But the play has one entire Act to go. Act 5 is self-contained and intended to sustain audience interest by the wit and playful teasing of Bassanio and Gratiano by Portia and Nerissa.

There are two plots, Antonio's bond with Shylock to provide money for Bassanio and Portia's marriage. Initially, the first takes place in Venice and the second takes place in Belmont. These interlink from the start in the sense that Bassanio is borrowing money to finance his wooing of the beautiful and wealthy Portia, in the hopes of marrying her.

Still, these two plots provide the basis of Shakespeare's structure in the play as we move back and forth between the two stories and consequently between Venice and Belmont.

The real intersection between the two comes after Portia and Bassanio are married and Portia dresses as a man and comes to Venice to appear in the court. She transforms from woman to man and from Belmont to Venice. She successfully makes the transition on both levels.

The final Act of the play is in idyllic Belmont, removed from the troubles and conflict of Venice. These shifts in setting form the basis of Shakespeare's structure in *The Merchant of Venice*.

Humour

Humour is a technique that can have a profound effect on the tone of a scene and the effect of the whole play on the audience. This is especially true of *The Merchant of Venice*.

In Act 1 Scene 1, the idiosyncratic Salarino and Salario are amusing to the audience. Their presence and behaviour serve to lighten the tone of the first part of the scene, which is essentially about Antonio's melancholia (not usually a subject of humour.) It is worth noting that they don't actually tell any 'jokes', either, but rather create humour through their costumes perhaps, their general demeanour and stage business.

In fact, if we don't find them amusing enough, we will probably invent some suitable stage business to get the audience laughing. We want to do this without taking away the reality of Antonio's depression, the fact that he is sincerely unhappy.

Act 1 Scene 2 is set in Belmont where we find Portia and Nerissa discussing the (lack of) quality of the suitors that have come interested in her hand in marriage. In my view, this is the funniest written scene in the play.

The most important effect of the humour here will be to make the audience pleasantly disposed towards Portia. Audiences usually like characters that make them laugh. If we play up the humour in this scene, then it should play down the potential for the audience to see Portia as a 'princess' who thinks that no one is good enough for her. In fact, the suitors sound 'pretty crook' and the audience should be able to sympathise with her hope that someone better will come along.

When the Princes of Morocco and Arragon make their appearances to take their chances with the test of the caskets, each of them makes long speeches in preparing to make their selections. We can make these characters the objects of humour if we like, through casting and costuming and their manner of speaking. We can costume them as stereotypes, even anachronistic ones, for example dress Morocco as a 1970s disco dancer. The effect will be that if we make the audience laugh *at* them, they will not take them seriously as contenders for Portia's hand. This will also decrease any inclination to again view Portia as conceited or dishonest.

What the humour does, in these instances concerning Portia, is it aligns the audience with Portia by having the audience laugh at the same people about whom she is laughing, and rejecting.

Lancelot and Gobbo are stock comic characters who provide comic interludes for the audience. They are not important to the plot, except that Lancelot, by leaving Shylock to work for Bassanio, adds to the impression we get that Shylock is not a pleasant person to be around. But Lancelot's long soliloquy in Act 2 Scene 2 is also about the subject matter of the play – about Jews, stereotyping and tolerance. Interestingly, the simple Lancelot shows more of a conscience towards Shylock than do his more educated 'betters'. Here, Shakespeare is using humour as a way of examining an aspect of one of the main themes of the play.

The disguise is often a source of humour, and so it is in *The Merchant of Venice*. Towards the end of Act 4, Portia disguised as Balthasar and Nerissa disguised as 'his' clerk, each succeed in getting from their unsuspecting husbands, the rings that they had them promise never to remove.

This sets up the fun of Act 5 when Portia and Nerissa demand to know where the rings have gone. When Bassanio and Gratiano try to explain who they gave them to and why, Portia and Nerissa produce the rings, saying that they slept with the men that gave them to them. The audience knows that this means merely that they slept with themselves, but Gratiano declares that he and Bassanio have been 'cuckolded' when they themselves are innocent of such a crime. (A cuckold is a man whose wife is having affairs with other men.)

Just when things are on the verge of getting out of hand, Portia explains that they were in fact Balthasar and 'his' clerk, so that the rings had been given to their rightful owners anyway and are where they belong. She reserves a fuller explanation of events for some time, just as the play ends.

This scene is intended to be humorous in a teasing kind of way. The audience is supposed to enjoy Portia, again, holding the upper hand by knowing more than the other characters. It shows an assertive woman and a level of good-will and tolerance on the part of Bassanio especially. The scene might tell us something about love and the tests it can be put through. This relates to the device of the caskets. If it is, indeed, a test on their love, then their love survives the test well.

To summarise the main point – Shakespeare uses humour to entertain the audience, no one can deny that. But he uses it, as well, to enhance other things in the play – character exposition and themes.

In *The Merchant of Venice*, humour is very important in its effect on the overall tone of the play. The Shylock plot is a very serious business which involves very serious issues. That aspect of the play would not be played for laughs in a contemporary production. So, the humour elsewhere will balance the seriousness of the Shylock story. The question arises as to how you want to 'strike the balance'. Do you want the audience to leave the theatre laughing and full of delight for the future of these young lovers and Venetians? Or would you prefer your audience to leave the theatre with the suffering of Shylock foremost in their minds?

Humour is a technique that you will use to lighten the play, or use less if you wish to darken the play.

USE OF SYMBOLS

The Caskets

The caskets are the device developed by Portia's father that allow him to determine who she marries indirectly, and even after his own death.

They symbolise the world's view of value through their three differing materials – gold, silver and lead. They are an attempt to exploit the tendency of human beings to judge on the basis of appearance, of superficial qualities.

The test itself is a quest for Portia. It is a test of wisdom and the prize is Portia herself, represented by the portrait of her that is inside just one of them.

As they are vessels containing secrets, they symbolise Portia's sexuality. This is the ultimate, not articulated prize.

The Pound of Flesh

The pound of flesh is, of course, literal. It is a real pound of real flesh that Shylock is talking about cutting from Antonio's chest.

But it is also a powerful symbol, one that has become a part of our cultural memory and entered our language. The pound of flesh symbolises a debt. It is a powerful symbol because of its visceral nature. When we here Shylock say it, we imagine what it would be like to have the flesh cut out of you, or, indeed to do the cutting.

Not everyone has read or seen *The Merchant of Venice*, but everyone knows what it means to demand "one's pound of flesh". It is to stand for your right to hurt or harm someone else. It is an expression for doing the 'wrong thing', even when you are 'in the right' in doing it. It is an expression for vengeance.

Leah's Ring

This is only mentioned briefly in the play, but it is an image with a lasting impression. Amongst the jewellery that Jessica takes with her when she elopes is a ring which Shylock particularly mentions as having sentimental value because it was given to him by 'Leah' when he was a bachelor. It is generally presumed that Leah must be Jessica's mother. Tubal, Shylock's Jewish friend, tells him that one trader told him that Jessica had traded the ring for a monkey. Shylock is particularly upset by this, saying that he would never have traded it, even for 'a wilderness of monkeys'. (3.1.97)

The ring symbolises Shylock's family – himself, Leah and Jessica. It is this family that Jessica disregards if it is true that she has traded the ring for a monkey.

The most important effect of this symbol is that it arouses thoughts in the audience that tend to humanise Shylock. Suddenly he has a past – he used to be a bachelor, and in love! What happened to his wife, Jessica's mother? Does he still miss her? Did she die, or is it possible that she left him too?

That the ring has obvious sentimental value for him indicates that he has sentiments. This might come as a surprise to the audience.

One film version of *The Merchant of Venice* has as the final shot of the film, a shot of the ring, on Jessica's finger. This shot tells the audience that she did not, in fact, exchange it for a monkey, and that she hasn't forgotten her mother or her family. It is such a small moment in the film, but it even opens up the hope that she and Shylock will one day be reconciled. After all, they are now both Christians!

LANGUAGE FEATURES IN *THE MERCHANT OF VENICE*

In *The Merchant of Venice*, Shakespeare has the ladies and gentlemen of Venice and Belmont speak, as refined people, mostly in verse. That is, their speech is set out as poetry. This reflects their education and gentility. There are though, exceptions to this – in Act 1 Scene 2, Portia and Nerissa mock the suitors to Portia's heart in the natural language of prose.

'Low' characters Lancelot and Gobbo speak in prose, like ordinary sentences, to reflect their lack of refinement and education. When Lancelot speaks to Jessica, he speaks in prose and she answers in verse.

The interesting thing is that Shylock speaks in both prose and verse, suggesting that as a character, he exists in some nether region, neither one nor the other. This reflects his position in Venetian society. He, though, like the others, speaks in verse in the court scene.

The Language of The Test of the Caskets

Three men agree to take the challenge of the caskets in their quest to have Portia as their wife. In making their choice, they each make a speech of a high style, full of metaphor.

The Prince of Morocco

Morocco thinks aloud as he ruminates over his choice. 'This casket threatens' is an example of personification. (2.7.18) Its effect is to give animation and human qualities to the caskets. It is as though they deliberately bar him.

'A golden mind stoops not to shows of dross'. (2.7.20) Morocco regards himself as the 'golden mind', a metaphor that associates the value of gold with the mind of the Prince is so overblown that it suggests to the audience that he is mistaken in calling the lead 'dross'.

As he comes to the golden casket, his images become more grand and exotic – 'The Hyrcanian deserts' and 'the vasy wilds / Of wild Arabia'. Until, with certainty, he calls for the key with a forthright declaration: 'Deliver me the key' (2.7.59)

Arragon

He rejects gold, because of 'the fool multitude'. (2.9.25) This is a metaphor which turns many (multitude) into one (fool). The image denigrates the many by reducing it to one and allowing it merely the intelligence of the fool. He also calls the people 'the barbarous multitudes' (2.9.32), they are uncivilised as well as foolish.

He continues his imagery of disdain for society with 'and how much honour / Picked from the chaff and ruin of the times / To be new varnished!' (2.9.46) Honour is objectified and gleaned from the unclean state of things. 'Picked' is denigrating and the metaphor 'new varnished' suggests a superficiality to the honour.

Bassanio

Bassanio begins by characterising the world as 'still deceived with ornament.' (3.2.74) He uses the metaphor of appearance and reality represented by a corrupt plea spoken in a gracious voice.'

The word 'seasoned' is suggestive of artificial or not natural flavour.

'This ornament is but the guiled shore / To a most dangerous sea' (3.2.96) again contrasts appearance with reality, using a metaphor based on safety at sea, a motif in the play. He follows this with the alliteration of 'gaudy gold' with its rhythm that tends to denigrate. Gold is 'gaudy', bright on the outside, showy. Thus he chooses the lead and has the woman.

Shylock's speech 3.1.42-57

Shylock begins with the effect called 'accumulation' as he gains momentum through 'He hath disgraced me, and hindered me half a million, laughed at my losses' (line 43) and so on. Accumulation works, because it piles example upon example until the sheer weight of them carries the argument.

Then he embarks upon a series of rhetorical questions, starting with 'and what's his reason?' (line 46)

He delivers the answer to the first rhetorical question with a simple bluntness – 'I am a Jew.' (line 46) The use of a short sentence is abrupt, it pulls the reader/audience up. The rhetorical questions that follow have an implied answer of 'yes, of course'. The audience quickly concedes that Jews have eyes, and so on.

There is an even greater cumulative effect with these. They lead all the way to death, but that is not where Shylock leaves it. By asking about revenge, he points out that the Christians have been taking revenge on the Jews for generations. 'Revenge' is powerful in a single-word sentence.

'The villainy you teach me I will execute, and it shall go hard but I will better the instruction.' (3.1.56-7) The word 'execute' echoes in the audience's minds because it is a pun with two meanings. The word 'instruction' refers to being taught, but combined with the word 'better' it sets up an irony, that 'better' will be far worse.

Shakespeare's characters are what they say. And, they express themselves in a most metaphorical way. Did real people ever speak in this way? Probably not, but the language used by a Shakespeare character often has a resonance that means that what is said has a significance in general life as well as within the theatre and to the specific situation or character in the play.

THE ESSAY

The essay consists of the basic form of an introduction, body paragraphs and conclusion. The esssay has been the subject of numerous texts and you should have the basic form well in hand. As teachers, the point we would emphasise would be to link the paragraphs both to each other and back to your argument (which should directly respond to the question). Of course, ensure your argument is logical and sustained.

Make sure you use specific examples and that your quotes are accurate. To ensure that you respond to the question, make sure you plan carefully and are sure what relevant point each paragraph is making. It is solid technique to actually 'tie up' each point by explicitly coming back to the question.

When composing an essay the basic conventions of the form are:

> - State your argument, outline the points to be addressed and perhaps have a brief definition.

A solid structure for each paragraph is:
- Topic sentence (*the main idea and its link to the previous paragraph/ argument*)
- Explanation/ discussion of the point including links between texts if applicable.
- Detailed evidence (*Close textual reference – quotes, incidents and technique discussion.*)
- Tie up by restating the point's relevance to argument/ question

> - Summary of points
> - Final sentence that restates your argument

As well as this basic structure, you will need to focus on:

Audience – for the essay the audience must be considered formal unless specifically stated otherwise. Therefore, your language must reflect the audience. This gives you the opportunity to use the jargon and vocabulary that you have learnt in English. For the audience ensure your introduction is clear and has impact. Avoid slang or colloquial language including contractions (like 'doesn't', 'e.g.', 'etc.').

Purpose – the purpose of the essay is to answer the question given. The examiner evaluates how well you can make an argument and understand the module's issues and its text(s). An essay is solidly structured so its composer can analyse ideas. This is where you earn marks. It does not retell the story or state the obvious.

Communication – Take a few minutes to plan the essay. If you rush into your answer it is almost certain you will not make the most of the brief 40 minutes to show all you know about the question. More likely you will include irrelevant details that do not gain you marks but waste your precious time. Remember an essay is formal so **do not** do the following: story-tell, list and number points, misquote, use slang or colloquial language, be vague, use non-sentences or fail to address the question.

PLAN:

Don't even think about starting without one!

Introduce...

the texts you are using in the response

Argument: The human experience is affected by:

- Idea One
- Idea Two
- Idea Three

You need to let the marker know what texts you are discussing. You can start with a definition but it can come in the first paragraph of the body. You MUST state your argument in response to the question and the points you will cover as part of it. Wait until the end of the response to give it!

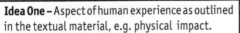

Idea One – Aspect of human experience as outlined in the textual material, e.g. physical impact.

Idea Two – Another aspect of human experience as outlined in the textual material, e.g. psychological impact.

- explain the idea
- where and how is it shown in the prescribed text?
- where and how is it shown in related text 1?

Idea Three – People's sense of experience is affected by context and environment

- explain the idea
- where and how shown in the prescribed text?
- where and how shown in related text 1?

You can use the things you have learned to organise the essay. For each one, you say where you saw this in your prescribed text and where in related text(s).

Two or three ideas are usually enough as you can explore them in detail.

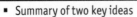

- Summary of two key ideas
- Final sentence that restates your argument

Make sure your conclusion restates your argument. It does not have to be too long.

MODEL ESSAY OUTLINE

> **To what extent are human experiences significant in the set text?**
>
> **From your studies respond to this question using your set text and at ONE piece of other textual material**

This essay needs to be attacked in a manner that responds to the question and shows ALL your knowledge about the text. The question lends itself to a close study of William Shakespeare's *The Merchant of Venice* as the text does show how the human experience is integral to life and how it shapes our other experiences and interaction with the world.

An introduction might be written:

> Human experiences are important in Shakespeare's play *The Merchant of Venice* and the two related texts, Lawrence's film *Jindabyne* and Ed Sheeran's song *Castle on the Hill*. These texts show how human experiences are integral to human existence and bring more meaning to one's life. Life is about experiences that challenge us and define how we see the world. They shape our beliefs and attitudes and can be confronting at the same time. Without experiences our lives would be empty and meaningless.

Your essay should then follow the outlined plan and develop these ideas. This gives you the opportunity to link the texts and fully develop each of the ideas.

ANNOTATED RELATED MATERIAL: DIFFERENT STUDIES OF HUMAN EXPERIENCES

Jindabyne – Ray Lawrence

Jindabyne is an Australian film that captures a wide array of human experiences. It touches on the ideas mentioned in the introduction to this text in a number of detailed instances. We can begin by considering the following before beginning a detailed examination of the narrative.

The collective human experience:

- Aboriginality and the spiritual;
- The Fishermen and their code;
- The reaction of the townsfolk;
- Media response;
- Interaction with the natural world.

Individual Experience:

- An individual character's response to the body – choose one;
- The killer;
- Response to the revelations;
- Past experiences and how they impact on current experiences;
- Reaction to loss – emotional;
- Assumptions about life.

We can now look at the plot to help us understand each of these issues. *Jindabyne* begins with the sound of a radio being tuned and the Australian feel of the movie is immediate with the theme music for the ABC news. Lawrence emphasises the isolation by having the radio not tune in correctly for an unknown female character, forcing her to use the cassette player. With this unusual beginning we know that her experience is not going to be positive.

We then pan to the rocks slowly where Gregory, our killer, sits patiently in a truck with the engine running watching the road. We know he is prepared for this as he has binoculars. He sees an Aboriginal girl, Susan O'Connor, driving and she is the one fiddling with the radio. He chases her down and forces her to stop. He moves toward her as we see a long shot of how isolated they are. We see his face in her window looming above her and screaming about the electricity coming down from the mountains. This film is no murder mystery, as we know from the beginning that the murderer is Gregory the electrician. This is about the experiences of the other characters in the film and how they respond to current experiences.

The Kane family, Stewart, Claire and son Tom, is waking. Claire pretends to sleep, before waking suddenly and being affectionate with Tom. Stewart and Tom head out fishing. The scene doesn't feel quite right and there is some emotional tension between Stewart and Claire that is unspoken due to what they have experienced in the past. Claire had a complicated past when she was pregnant with Tom. When she finds she is pregnant again, she becomes emotional and slightly unstable.

As the film builds we see the complex pasts of the characters and their interactions in the confinement of the small town. The fishing trip is a break from this and extremely important in their lives.

We see some of the emotional instability in characters such as Caylin-Calandria, who with Tom, has some issues at school. Along with Caylin-Calandria, Claire and Jude also have issues but in a nicely framed shot of the three female characters, we see them conform as members of a close knit group. The sacrifice they make is similar to Gregory's but on a different scale. Note the connection here and how each one is to get back to order and societal norms. This is the collective experience for all the characters.

At the Kanes' home the tensions are obvious from their past experiences but they contain it for appearances' sake. Occasionally, the tension reaches breaking point and the experience strains the superficial approach. The tension builds at home and the fishing trip seems like a good opportunity to break the cycle.

When we see Gregory dump Susan O'Connor's body in the river, we know that the fishing and her death will interact.

The next morning, the fishermen head off for their one big trip of the year and the sign 'Gone fishing' is put in the garage window. We see Billy on the phone to Elissa and putting the sign the wrong way round in the window shows his immaturity. They have already said they are taking him away to make a man of him. The four men have a few beers on the way and talk as they travel through the landscape. They intend to give Billy the experience they think he needs as a 'man' — a cultural rite of passage.

The men arrive and the high-tension electricity wires punctuate the wilderness. They begin to hike toward the valley. It's a long walk in and the terrain is hilly and difficult. They stop on the way and again we see Billy's naivety when Stewart says 'Listen to that' meaning the silence but he can't, as he has his earphones in. It is part of the break in tension of the film that they commune with nature. This experiential break affects all the men. The episode represents a distinct human experience.

Stewart wanders down the river fishing and sees Susan's body caught in the rocks. Hesitantly, he wades out to it and turns it over saying 'Oh Jesus' repeatedly. He screams for the others to come as he drags the body to the bank. He is obviously upset, making the sign of the cross. Stewart tells Rocco to 'take her, for fuck's sake, take her' and their shock is obvious. They all stare at the body and Billy goes to run off but they stop him. The four men meet and decide to leave her in the water and tie her so she doesn't float away.

The presence of the body threatens to detract from the enjoyment of the fishing experience. The act of attempted isolation of the bad experience is expected to evoke only a mild response. They do not anticipate the stormy reaction it receives when they return to the community.

The men go on fishing, with Stewart getting the first big fish on an absolutely perfect day. The lure of the fish is strong, especially when they see the big one he has caught. They have a successful and enjoyable time, a positive experience. They get a photo of the catch and Billy holds up his fish in a typical hunter/gatherer pose. Capturing an experience this way is most enjoyable.

It is a photo that will come back to haunt them as things change back in the world. An unanticipated adverse reaction can be a horrific experience.

Stewart goes to check on the dead girl, rolling her over and getting debris off her face in a quite tender gesture. The next day they head back and report it. At the car Billy rings Elissa and says they found a body but 'caught the most amazing fish'. They are told by the police to wait and seem despondent their trip has been ruined. They organise their story as Stewart says they have 'to get their story straight'.

We cut to Gregory eating breakfast and he appears to be a normal, lonely man until he goes out to his shed where he has hidden Susan's car and this reminds us of the evil in him. Consider his experience and his motivations. How does he see his actions and the world?

The next day at the station the policeman tells the fishermen 'we don't step over bodies for our recreational pursuits' and 'the whole town's ashamed of you'. When they are told to 'piss off' from the station the press are waiting for them and Billy makes a comment. Carl is angry with the press but we can begin to see signs of distress within the whole group.

The experience they had so looked forward to has become a negative one and the tensions we saw before are exacerbated by the emotional and collective response to the murder. Claire soon becomes obsessed with the whole affair because of her own state. The newspaper the next day has the headline, 'Men fish over dead body' because Billy has talked. Billy is late to work and Stewart tells him they have to 'stick together on this'.

Susan's sister calls them 'animals' and raises the race question by asking if they would have left a white girl. The Aboriginal youths begin to attack and vandalise the property of the men in violent outbursts, including throwing a rock through Billy's van window and thus endangering his baby. They insult Carl at the caravan park and vandalise the garage.

The police aren't any help and the situation deteriorates. Jude tells the police they shouldn't be enforcing the 'political correctness' laws. The intervention of the sense of Aboriginality and race challenges the assumptions people have and how we see the world. The contrasting views are ingrained in the social structures and part of different collective experiences.

The Aboriginal people see the white people as 'interfering' and the group of fishermen begin to fight amongst themselves. Elissa says they shouldn't go to the bush at all as it's sacred. The group talk about the bush and Rocco punches Stewart for saying the Aborigines are superstitious. The experience of racial tension becomes ever-present and adds to the emotional responses to the experience.

We now head slowly to a resolution of the conflict brought about by the various experiences. Each is handled in a different manner by characters and you can explore one or two of the responses. To cycle back to the original murder, Claire is stalked by Gregory in his truck. He stops her but drives off after staring weirdly, an odd experience in itself.

Terry and Stewart talk and Stewart meets Rocco and Carl. He tells them Claire's left him 'again'. Rocco can't believe it and we cross cut to her looking out into the wilderness after he looks thoughtfully out the window. These different reactions to experiences mirror attitudes in life and reactions to emotional and intellectual conflict.

In conclusion, Lawrence takes us back to the healing power of nature in our human experiences when the Aboriginal people are having a ceremony. Gregory watches while Claire walks in. Again we see his truck as an omnipresent force in the film, almost an extension of him. An Aboriginal man tells Claire to 'piss off' from the ceremony after she says she has come to pay her 'respects' but he is told to leave her alone by an Auntie.

The smoke and tribal music symbolise the ceremonial nature of the setting and the camera pans around the scene and the bush. We see parts of the ceremony with chanting and clapping sticks. The camera moves in and out while other shots pan around the bush, giving us the full experience and Lawrence portrays this as a positive, healing experience.

Eventually Stewart, Tom, Carl, Jude and Rocco arrive to pay respects. Tom runs to his mother and Stewart goes over and says 'Sorry' but is rebuffed by the father who throws dirt on him and spits, refusing his apology. Then an Aboriginal girl tells a little about Susan's story and sings the last love song Susan wrote.

The camera pans around all the faces as they listen to the song and the ceremonial smoke wafts around. It seems to have some healing effect on everyone, as it is a meaningful experience which raises the idea of the spiritual experience in the text. The girl stops singing through emotion. 'Be gone' seems to symbolise in language the whole scenario for each character.

We see a long wide shot of the bush before fading back to Gregory waiting again in his car behind the rocks for another victim. It is quite a circular conclusion and it is an odd end when he crushes the fly. We don't quite know what to make of the whole experience and he seems to be the only character unchanged by the experiences in the film.

Poem: 'Inland' by John Kinsella

The poem captures the mood and ethos of the outback farming communities and deals with the human aspect more than some of the other poems in Kinsella's collection: *Peripheral Light*. This poem is one long restless thought that mimics memories and recollection while raising the current, topical issues that concern the poet. As usual with his poems Kinsella orientates the audience early with the word 'Inland' and then continues the poem without a full stop. The poem flows with the use of commas but Kinsella allows us to stop and think with the use of the colon, brackets and the hyphen. Look for these punctuation stops as you read as they emphasise a specific point or idea that resonates with the audience.

The first stanza gives us a foreshadowing of the events to follow with the warnings in the words 'storm', 'alert' and 'uncertain'. This ominous tone is reinforced by the word 'ghosts' and the implication of death which is constant in much of Kinsella's poetry. The next stanza deals with a more human element and we get the country feel with the bracketed gossip about McHenry's accident which shows the close knit community. Habits here are formed as part of survival and known to all as we see 'the old man plying the same track' and the families possibly heading to church on the Sunday morning.

The third stanza returns to the vagaries of nature. Kinsella repeats 'uncertain' with regard to the weather. Weather and the environment play a large role in farming communities and it is especially so at sowing and harvest. Despite the uncertainty and 'ashen' days which alter 'moods', the community returns to their habits and routines which shape their lives. The next stage returns to the road and the implication of a journey but a journey that is straight and in conflict with the cycles of the natural world. The path seems already marked and measured. It is 'straight and narrow', marked by a theodolite.

The final four lines of the poem are pure Kinsella, marking the transience of humanity on the landscape. We read

> 'it's a place of borrowed dreams
> where the marks of the spirit
> have been erased by dust –
> the restless topsoil'

The European farmers had 'borrowed dreams' for their own relationship with the land but this line also harks back to the indigenous Dreamtime when the land was created. The indigenous view that the land owns the people is also true for Kinsella. This sense of nobody owning the land is strong in his poetry. European impact on the land can be seen in the spirituality being removed by the dust—dust created by the poor farming techniques transferred from a different land. He finishes with the 'restless topsoil' as if the whole earth is moving in its own discontented journey, just as the people move.

The influence here of genuinely lost spirituality and connection with the land as we move directly on the 'high road' contrasts with the more flowing, 'restless' side of the natural world. This visual contrast is obvious but we can also discuss the contrast between habit and spirit. 'Inland' is a poem that uses the landscape to show the contrast between two views of the countryside.

DRAMA: Eugene O'Neil's *Desire Under the Elms*

O'Neill sets out to instruct how the house and elms should appear and the year is 1850. Note how he describes the 'enormous' elms as,

> 'exhausted women resting their sagging breasts and hands and hair on its roof, and when it rains their tears trickle down monotonously and rot on the shingles'

and how they dominate and 'rot'. It is important to read this both in terms of the play and in the context of American theatre. The description here shows O'Neill's genius at new design and original theatricality.

Part One: Scene One

The whole first page and a third are nearly all playwright notes that describe the farm, the house and the characters of Eben, Simeon and Peter. The first words of the play, 'God! Purty!' reflect the beauty of the land and how Eben perceives it. Eben is 'resentful and defensive' and feels 'trapped' on the farm.

His older half-brothers Simeon and Peter are 'more bounce and homelier in face, shrewder and more practical.' They all have worked hard on their father's farm over the years and have little feeling for their absent father. We learn that Simeon had a 'woman' who died and that Peter is excited by the prospect of 'gold in the West'. They all talk about how hard they've worked and hope that the father might 'die soon'. What we get from all this is that they are earthy and this is reflected in their bodies and clothes which are all dirt stained.

We also see here the difference between them as Eben sees gold in the pasture, not California, as they head in for a dinner of bacon in what seems a ritual they have performed many times before. Note that O'Neill calls for the use of the curtain at the end of the scene.

Scene Two

It is twilight and again we get detailed notes on the interior scene. Simeon tells Eben he should not wish their father dead and Eben replies he's not his son but, 'I'm Maw – every drop of blood!' He then blames the father, Ephraim Cabot, for killing his mother by working her to death but the others just say there was work to be done. O'Neill gets them to list the jobs and Eben comes back with 'vengeful passion' that, while they did nothing, he will see his mother gets 'rest and sleep in her grave!'

They then discuss Cabot's absence and how he just drove off in a buggy one day in a rush. Simeon says that when he went,

'He druv off in the buggy, all spick an' span, with the mare all breshed an' shiny, druv off clackin' his tongue an' wavin' his whip. I remember it quite well'

Eben mocks Simeon for not stopping him and the scene concludes with Eben leaving to see Minnie the town whore. We learn all the Cabot men have slept with her. Simeon and Peter say that Eben is just like 'Paw' and thinks of California. The final image is of Eben with his arms stretched to the sky talking about starts and sin, 'my sin's as purty as any one on 'em!', until he 'strides' to the village for Min.

Scene Three

It is 'pitch darkness' and Eben comes home with the news that Cabot has married a 'purty' thirty-five year old. He has heard this in the village and this effectively disinherits the boys. Simeon and Peter see California as their only option now. Eben tells the boys that they can have three hundred dollars each if they sign their share of the farm over to him. He can get the money as his mother told him,

> 'I know whar it's hid. I been waitin' – Maw told me. She knew whar it lay fur years, but she was waitin'....It's her'n – the money he hoarded from her farm an' hid from Maw. It's my money by rights now.'

They think about it and Eben tells them about his night with Min. He tells how he hates the new wife after the boys suggest he might sleep with her, just like Min, to get the old man back. Peter and Simeon say they'll do the deal and leave the farm. Both are bitter and vindictive about Cabot.

Scene Four

The setting is the same as Scene Two and the boys are discussing how they don't have to work now – it is all down to Eben who is jubilant as he thinks it will all be his. Peter and Simeon again reflect on how like his father he is, 'Like his Paw'. They also tell he isn't much of a milker but they soon talk about their leaving and how they'll miss some aspects of the farm.

Eben comes back in and says that the 'old mule an the bride' are coming. The two older boys begin to pack and sign Eben's papers as he gives them the money Cabot had hidden. They tell him they'll send him 'a lump o' gold for Christmas' and head into the yard feeling 'light' because of their newfound freedom.

Ephraim Cabot and Abbie Putnam then come in and O'Neill describes them in detail. Cabot is

> 'seventy-five, tall and gaunt, with great, wiry, concentrated power, but stoop shouldered by toil. His face is hard as if it were hewn from a boulder, yet there is a weakness in it'

but his face is weakened with petty pride. Abbie is

> 'thirty-five, buxom, full of vitality. Her round face is pretty but marred by its rather gross sensuality. There is strength and obstinacy in her jaw, a hard determination in her eyes, and about her whole personality.'

She also has a 'desperate quality'. Cabot shows Abbie the place and she says to him it's 'mine'. Then he sees the two boys not working. He introduces Abbie and she goes to look at 'her' house and they warn her Eben's inside.

Cabot tells them to get to work and they give him cheek, saying they are 'free' and heading to California. They 'whoop' it up and he says he'll have them chained up. They throw rocks at the house, smashing the window and head off singing. Abbie sticks her head out the window and says she likes the room but he is thinking of the stock and 'almost runs' to the barn.

Abbie then meets Eben in the kitchen and talks to him in 'seductive tones'. She says she doesn't want to be his 'Maw' but friends and he cusses her. She tells him of her troubled life and how Cabot gave her a chance to escape it. He calls her a 'harlot' and they argue over ownership of the farm. She has the upper hand in law and he leaves but the seeds of their growing attraction have been set.

Outside he and his father argue about life and work and he tells Eben 'Ye'll never be more'n half a man!' The scene ends with Abbie washing up and the faint notes of the song the boys were singing as they left.

Part Two: Scene One

Again O'Neill describes in detail the farmhouse setting. Two months have passed and it is a hot Sunday afternoon. Abbie in her best outfit is sitting on the porch and Eben comes out of the house also dressed in his best. They stalk each other, both attracted and repelled. As he walks away she 'gives a sneering, taunting chuckle' at him and they argue but the attraction is obvious. She says that nature will pull him to her but he says that she is married and he goes to leave her.

She accuses him of going to Min and she gets angry stating he'll never get the farm,

> 'Ye'll never live t' see the day when even a stinkin' weed on it 'll belong t' ye!'

He says he hates her and leaves as Cabot enters. She tells him Eben has been mocking him and twists the conversation to the inheritance of the farm. She tells him Eben lusts after her and as he angers she backs off in her accusations. Reassured, he says that she can have the farm if she bears the son she says she wants with him. He says that he'd 'do anythin' ye axed, I tell ye!' if she gave him a son and tells her to pray to God for it to happen.

Scene Two

It is about eight in the evening and here the bedrooms are highlighted, with Eben in one and Cabot with Abbie in the other. The two of them are talking about a son. They seem together, yet apart, as he tells her of his life on the farm and how God's hard. He both lost and gained on the way through, but the farm is his. He says he is pleased he found her, his 'Rose o' Sharon'. Abbie promises him that she will bear a son as he basically threatens her,

> 'Ye don't know nothin' – nor never will. If ye don't hev a son t' redeem ye...'

and he leaves to sleep in the barn with the cows 'whar it's restful'.

We then see Eben and Abbie restless and she leaves the room and goes to him. He 'submits' to her kisses then 'hurls' her away. Abbie says she'd make him 'happy' and she knows he wants her too much. She tells him to go down to the parlour and he is shocked as this is where his mother was 'laid out'. She leaves for the parlour and he wonders what's happening. The scene closes with a question to his dead mother, 'Maw! Whar are yew?' but we know that he wants her and will go to her.

Scene Three

The scene now shifts to the parlour which is described as a 'grim, repressed room like a tomb'. Abbie waits and Eben appears and he sits at her invitation. They talk about his Maw and how they hate Cabot. Abbie throws herself at him with 'wild passion' and he is caught up in the moment and thinks that it's his Maw wanting him to sleep with Abbie to get revenge on Cabot,

I see it! I sees why. It's her vengeance on him – so's she kin rest quiet in her grave!

Abbie proclaims her love for him and he for her then they kiss 'in a fierce, bruising kiss' to close the scene.

Scene Four

A more bold and confident Eben leaves the house and Abbie opens the parlour window. She calls him over for a kiss and they talk a bit before Eben says his Maw can now rest. They split as Cabot comes out of the barn but are now obviously in love. Eben tells Cabot that his Maw is now at rest and Cabot says he rests best with the cows. Cabot is confused but the scene ends with him criticising Eben as 'Soft-headed' and a 'born fool' but, being a practical man, he heads for breakfast.

Part Three: Scene One

Time has passed to 'late spring the following year'. Eben is upstairs in emotional and psychological conflict while a party happens downstairs. Cabot has drunk too much and Abbie sits, pale and thin, in a rocking chair. There is a fiddler and Abbie begins the scene by asking for Eben and the guests 'titter' as most think the baby is Eben's, not Cabot's, which is true enough. They laugh and Cabot is angered by this and orders them to dance. The fiddler 'slyly' says they're waiting for Eben but Cabot mocks the boy and then ensues a bawdy conversation about his fertility,

> I got a lot in me – a hell of a lot – folks don't know on. Fiddle 'er up, durn ye! Give 'em somethin' t' dance t!'

The fiddler plays and they dance. Cabot joins in frantically and 'whoop(s)' it up. He exhausts the fiddler and pours whiskey. In the upstairs room Eben is looking at the baby. Abbie goes upstairs and Cabot leaves for outside, 'fresh air', as she has told him not to 'tech' her. The guests gossip after he goes and we see Eben and Abbie upstairs and she professes her love for him,

> 'Don't git feelin' low. I love ye, Eben. Kiss me.'

Cabot says he's going to rest in the barn. The scene concludes with the fiddler playing in celebration of 'the old skunk gittin' fooled!'

Scene Two

Eben is outside half an hour later and Cabot is coming back from the barn. Cabot tells him to get a woman inside and he might get a farm. Eben replies that this farm's his and Cabot mocks him. He tells her Abbie has been promised the farm for her son and Eben is angered thinking Abbie has tricked him.

Eben goes to kill her but Cabot is too strong for him and Abbie comes out to stop him choking Eben. Cabot tells him he's weak and goes inside to celebrate. Abbie tries to be tender with Eben but he rejects her and calls her a liar.

> 'Ye're nothin' but a stinkin' passel o' lies. Ye've been lyin'
> t' me every word ye spoke, day an' night, since we fust –
> done it. Ye've kept sayin' ye loved me....'

She says she loves him and tells him that the promise was made before they fell in love. He says he'll go to California.

They argue and he 'torturedly' says he wished the baby had never been born. Abbie is distraught and she says she'd kill the baby to prove her love for him. He says he won't listen to her but she calls after him that she can 'prove' she loves him and she 'kin do one thin' God does'. Abbie is desperate at the end of the scene.

Scene Three

It is now just before dawn and Eben is in the kitchen ready to leave. Abbie is near the cradle with 'her face full of terror'. She sobs but Cabot stirs and she goes to the kitchen and flings her arms around Eben, kissing him 'wildly'. She says 'I killed him' and he thinks she means Cabot but is horrified when she tells him it's the baby.

Eben states it was his baby and she says she loved it but loves him more. He is angered,

'Don't ye tech me! Ye're pizzen! How could ye – t' murder a pore little critter – Ye must've swapped yer soul t' hell!

and tells her that he is getting the Sheriff and heads, 'panting and sobbing' to town. She calls out to him that she loves him.

Scene Four

It is after dawn and Abbie is in the kitchen. Cabot wakes in his room and is concerned that he has woken late. He checks the baby and is proud it is quiet and asleep. He goes down to Abbie in the kitchen and she tells him the baby is dead. He runs to check and comes back down and asks 'why?'

In a rage she tells him it was Eben's son and that she loves Eben, not him. He blinks back a tear and then gets 'stony' so he can carry on and says he is going to get the Sheriff. Abbie tells him that Eben's already gone so that Cabot tells her he'll 'git t' wuk.' He then tells her he'd never have told and now he's going to be 'lonesomer'n ever!' Eben comes back and Cabot tells him to get off the farm.

Eben asks for her forgiveness and tells her he loves her. He says he realised he loved her at the Sheriff's and they have a chance to run away but Abbie says she'll take her punishment. Eben says he will share it with her and plans to tell the Sheriff they planned it together. They think they can stand it together and then Cabot comes back.

He goes into a long tirade and tells them how he's let the stock go and will burn the house down. He too plans to go to California but finds that Eben has gotten to his money first. Cabot says that this is a sign from God to him to stay and that 'God's hard an' lonesome!' At this point the Sheriff comes and Eben says he was involved with the baby's murder.

Cabot says 'Take 'em both' and leaves to get his stock. The sun is coming up and as they are led away Eben says the farm's 'Purty' and Abbie agrees. The Sheriff finishes the play with the line, 'It's a jim-dandy farm, no denyin'. Wish I owned it!'

OTHER RELATED TEXTS

Fiction / Non-fiction / Drama

- *Wonder* – R G Palacio
- *First they Killed My Father* – Luong Ung
- *The Graveyard Book* – Neil Gaiman
- *Looking for Alaska* – John Green
- *Eleanor and Park* by Rainbow Rowell
- *The Fault in Our Stars* – John Green
- *We All Fall Down* – Robert Cormier
- *The Old Man and the Sea* – Ernest Hemingway
- *The Fire Eaters* – David Almond
- *Ender's Game* – Orson Scott Card
- *Hatchet* – Gary Paulsen
- *Inside Black Australia* – Kevin Gilbert
- *Sapiens: A Brief History of Humankind* – Yuval Noah Harari
- *Peeling the Onion* – Wendy Orr
- *Raw* – Scott Monk
- *Six Degrees of Separation* – John Guare
- *The Book Thief* – Markus Zusak
- *When Dogs Cry* – Markus Zusak
- *Holes* – Louis Sachar
- *The Outsiders* – S.E. Hinton
- *Roll of Thunder, Hear My Cry* – Mildred D. Taylor
- *A Small Free Kiss in the Dark* – Glenda Millard
- *Monster* – Walter Dean Myers
- *Lord of the Flies* – William Golding
- *Jandamarra* – Steve Hawke
- *A Separate Peace* – John Knowles
- *A Monster Calls* – Patrick Ness
- *The Pigman* – Paul Zindel
- *The Invention of Hugo Cabret* – Brian Selznik

- *Emerald City* – David Williamson
- *Silent Spring* – Rachel Carson

Films and Television

- *The Human Experience* – Charles Kinnane
- *My Brilliant Career* – Gillian Armstrong
- *Broadchurch* – James Strong & Euros Lyn
- *Twinsters* – Samantha Futerman and Ryan Miyamoto
- *Be My Brother* – Genevieve Clay - Smith
- *What's Eating Gilbert Grape* – Lasse Hallstrom
- *Pleasantville* – Gary Ross
- *Eternal Sunshine of the Spotless Mind* – Michel Gondry
- *Taxi Driver* – Martin Scorsese
- *Tootsie* – Sydney Pollack
- *Back in Time for Dinner* – Kim Maddever
- *The Godfather* – Francis Ford Coppola
- *Friends* – David Crane and Marta Kaufmann
- *Dawson's Creek* – Kevin Williamson
- *Orange is the New Black* – Jenji Kohan
- *Boy Meets World* – Michael Jacobs and April Kelly

Website – quote on literature and the human experience

*http://view2.fdu.edu/academics/university-college/school-of-humanities/
english-language-and-literature-program/*

At its most fundamental level literature explores what it means to be a human being in this world and tries to describe what our human experience is like. As such, literature pushes us to confront the large human questions that have plagued humankind for centuries: issues of fate and free will, issues relating to our role in the universe, our relationship to God, and our relationships with others. Studying literature not only helps us to understand the complexity of these questions intellectually, but because of its very nature, it allows us to experience these tensions vicariously. Literature does not just tell us about human experience; it recreates it in a way we can feel and visualise. In other words, it calls for a total response from us—it stretches us beyond who we are.

First, literature can enhance our ability to relate to people. Because literature focuses on human relationships and self perception, it can broaden our own experience—to help us understand different kinds of people, different cultures, different problems—and, consequently, help us better understand our own relationships with others.

The study of literature also helps to foster an appreciation for beauty, symmetry, and order. This means more than the intuitive response of liking or disliking something we see or read or hear; it means a carefully thought-through response that will enhance appreciation—not destroy it.

Perhaps the most important skills that the study of literature teaches are analytic and synthetic skills. In learning to read carefully and analytically, we learn to ask hard questions both of the work and of ourselves. And as we seek to discover the relationships between the ideas and images we uncover in a work, our ultimate goal is to see the whole—to see how the parts work together to make the piece what it is. In grappling with the complex and difficult ideas contained in literature, we learn to accept the multiple dimensions and ambiguity that are so often present in life.

Finally, the study of literature will also help develop our writing abilities as we come to value the written word and understand its power to communicate.

Beyond all of these skills, however, it is not what literature can do for us as individuals as much as what it can do to us. Literature speaks to the whole person. Listen to it, says C. S. Lewis, and you will be changed.

Poetry

- 'Warren Pryor' – Alden Nowlan
- 'The Gardener' – Louis MacNeice
- 'The Improvers' – Colin Thiele

Songs

- *Be My Escape* – Relient K
- *Mandolin Wind* – Rod Stewart
- *Roxanne* – The Police
- *Wake Me Up When September Ends* – Green Day
- *Under Pressure* – Queen & David Bowie
- *Candle in the Wind* – Elton John
- *Empire State of Mind* – Alicia Keys
- *Gold Digger* – Kanye West
- *We Are Young* – Fun.
- *Centrefold* – J. Geils Band
- *It's Time* – Imagine Dragons
- *We Cry* – The Script
- *If I Were a Boy* – Beyoncé
- *Shake it Out* – Florence + the Machine
- *C'mon* – Panic! At the Disco & Fun.
- *I Don't Love You* – My Chemical Romance
- *Sing* – My Chemical Romance
- *1985* – Bowling for Soup
- *What About Me* – Shannon Noll
- *Sinner* – Jeremy Loops
- *7 Years* – Lucas Graham

- *Bitter Sweet Symphony* – The Verve
- *Ghost!* – Kid Kudi
- *Good Riddance (Time of Your Life)* – Green Day
- *Expectations* – Belle and Sebastian
- *After Hours* – We Are Scientists
- *Write About Love* – Belle and Sebastian
- *Trust Your Stomach* – Marching Band
- *Heaven Knows I'm Miserable Now* – The Smiths